JAPANESE ARCHITECTURE
A SHORT HISTORY

Yo ni furu wa
Sara ni shigure no
Yadori ka na.
Truly man's living in this world
Is but a shelter from a shower.

Tzu Hsia, the disciple of Confucius, said: "The inferior man always embellishes his mistakes."

JAPANESE ARCHITECTURE

A SHORT HISTORY

A. L. Sadler

With a new foreword
by **Mira Locher**

TUTTLE PUBLISHING
Tokyo • Rutland, Vermont • Singapore

... us Editions (HK) Ltd., with
... endon, Vermont 05759 U.S.A.

... be reproduced or utilized in
..., including photocopying,
... al system, without prior writ-

Library of Congress Cataloging-in-Publication Data

Sadler, A. L. (Arthur Lindsay), b. 1882.
  [Short history of Japanese architecture]
  Japanese architecture : a short history / by A.L. Sadler.
      p. cm.
  Originally published: A short history of Japanese architecture, 1963.
  Includes bibliographical references.
  ISBN 978-4-8053-1043-4 (pbk.)
  1. Architecture--Japan--History. I. Title.
  NA1550.S25 2009
  720.952--dc22

                          2009000013

  ISBN 978-4-8053-1043-4

  Distributed by

  North America, Latin America & Europe
  Tuttle Publishing
  364 Innovation Drive
  North Clarendon, VT 05759-9436 U.S.A.
  Tel: 1 (802) 773-8930; Fax: 1 (802) 773-6993
  info@tuttlepublishing.com
  www.tuttlepublishing.com

  Japan
  Tuttle Publishing
  Yaekari Building, 3rd Floor
  5-4-12 Osaki
  Shinagawa-ku
  Tokyo 141 0032
  Tel: (81) 3 5437-0171; Fax: (81) 3 5437-0755
  tuttle-sales@gol.com

  Asia Pacific
  Berkeley Books Pte. Ltd.
  61 Tai Seng Avenue #02-12
  Singapore 534167
  Tel: (65) 6280-1330; Fax: (65) 6280-6290
  inquiries@periplus.com.sg
  www.periplus.com

  13 12 11 10 09   10 9 8 7 6 5 4 3 2 1

  Printed in Singapore

  TUTTLE PUBLISHING® is a registered trademark of Tuttle Publishing,
  a division of Periplus Editions (HK) Ltd.

CONTENTS

List of Illustrations 6

Foreword.. 12

Preface.. 22

CHAPTER 1: Introduction 23

CHAPTER 2: Early Period (660 B.C.- A.D. 540).............................. 30

CHAPTER 3: The Introduction Of Buddhism. Asuka Period
(540-640 A.D.) 37

CHAPTER 4: Hakuhō Period (640-720 A.D.) 42

CHAPTER 5: Tempyo Period (720-780 A.D.) 44

CHAPTER 6: Heian Period (780-1190 A.D.) 49

CHAPTER 7: Kamakura Period (1190-1340 A.D.)............................ 61

CHAPTER 8: Muromachi Period (1340-1570 A.D.) 69

CHAPTER 9: Momoyama Period (1570-1616 A.D.) 76

CHAPTER 10: Edo Period (1616-1860 A.D.) 89

CHAPTER 11: The Shogun's Reception Of The Emperor............. 108

CHAPTER 12: Building Regulations In The Tokugawa Period 110

CHAPTER 13: Shōji, Fusuma, And Ceilings 113

CHAPTER 14: Privy And Bathroom 116

CHAPTER 15: The Kitchen.. 120

CHAPTER 16: The Architect 122

Appendixes

1 Professor Amanuma's Illustrations Of Japanese Architecture
(Nippon Kenchikushi Zuroku).. 127

2 Comparative Table Of Dates.. 138

3 Glossary of Architectural Terms... 139

4 Bibliography.. 145

Plates 148

Endnotes.. 277

Index 282

LIST OF ILLUSTRATIONS

1. Forms of ancient houses.
2. Fig. 1. Plan of Izumo shrine.
   Fig. 2. Plan of Otori shrine.
   Fig. 3. Plan of Sumiyoshi shrine.
   Fig. 4. Umbrella shape plan of early house.
   Fig. 5. Conjectured most ancient form of house called Tenchi Kongen Miya-zukuri.
   Fig. 6. The Great Shrine of Izumo.
3. Fig. 1. The Ise Daijingu or Main Shrine at Ise.
   Fig. 2. Ordinary Shimmei style shrine.
4. The Sumiyoshi shrine.
5. Fig. 1. Kokuchu Sumai house in Iga district of Shiga prefecture.
   Fig. 2. Old house in Amatsu village.
   Fig. 3. House at Shirakawa, Hida province.
6. Fig. 1. House in Tansei village.
   Fig. 2. Old house in Iwakura village.
7. Sites of the ancient capitals in Yamato.
8. The capital of Asuka. Imperial mausolea.
9. Pillars of Asuka, Haku-ho, Tempyo, and Konin eras (590-824 A.D.).
10. Pillars of Fujiwara and Kamakura periods (824-1392 A.D.).
11. Pillars of Muromachi, Momoyama and Edo periods (1392-1868).
12. Elbow brackets (single, double, and triple).
13. Elbow brackets (sextuple, quintuple, septuple, groups of three, and close grouping).
14. Frog-crotches of Asuka, Heian, Muromachi, and Momoyama periods.
15. Fig. 1. Tail rafter bracket-supports, Kamakura period.
    Figs. 2-5. King-post construction of Kamakura and later periods.
16. Fig. 1. Relic casket in the shape of a tope from Manikyala, first century A.D.
    Fig. 2. Bracket capital of the fifth century at Nassick.
    Fig. 3. Pillar and capital of the fifth century at Ajanta.
    Fig. 4. Lotus and water-pot capital of India.
    Fig. 5. Palace façade at Barhut, showing pipal leaf window arches.
    Fig. 6. Bracket and strut construction of eleventh century at Mount Abu.
    Fig. 7. Nepalese Dagoba,
    Fig. 8. Wooden Jaina temple at Canara.
17. Fig. 1. Professor Amanuma's restoration of the Rondo of the Hōryuji.
    Fig. 2. Section of the cloister gallery of the Hōryuji.

18. The Kondo of the Hōryuji, elevation and section.

19. The five-storied pagoda of the Hōryuji.

20. Elbow brackets of the earliest period. Hōryuji temple, seventh century.

21. Fig. 1. Kudara style, Hōryuji type.

    Fig. 2. Kudara style, Shitennōji type.

    Fig. 3. Kara style (Nara), T'ang.

    Fig. 4. Zen style (Kamakura), Sung.

22. The capital of Heijo at Nara.

23. Pagoda of the Yakushiji temple.

24. Figs 1 and 2. Three-branch bracketing of the pagoda of the Yakushiji.

    Fig. 3. Pierced iron "spray" of the pinnacle of the Yakushiji pagoda.

    Fig. 4. Large and small capitals of the bracketing of the above.

25. Fig. 1. Plan of the Hōryuji temple.

    Fig. 2. Plan of the Tōdaiji temple as it was in the Tempyo era (729-748).

26. The Toshōdaiji. Kondo, section, detail of bracketing and side view.

27. Yume-dono of the Hōryuji temple, with its water-pot pinnacle.

28. The Imperial Storehouse of the Tōdaiji, called Shōsōin.

29. Fig. 1. Professor Amanuma's restoration of the seven-story pagoda of the
    Tōdaiji.

    Fig. 2. Hokkedo of the Tōdaiji.

30. The Heian capital. Plan showing the location of the Imperial City, the
    Palace, the Hōraku-in, the Hassho-in, the University, the Shinsen-en park,
    the markets, the Saiji and the Toji.

31. The Heian capital. Figs 1-3. Lay-outs of blocks of thirty-two rows.

    Fig. 4. Lay-out of the eastern market.

    Fig. 5. The Shishinden or throne hall with the Nan-en or southern court in
    front of it.

32. The Heian capital. The Dai-Dairi or Imperial City with the palace, the
    Hasshōin and Hōgakuin halls of ceremony, the eight departments of State,
    and the various palace and government offices. Kōnin period (810-824).

33. The Heian capital. Imperial palace (plan).

34. The Heian capital. The Chōdōin or Hasshōin, and the Hōgakuin, within the
    Imperial City.

35. The Heian capital. The plan of the Seiryōden of the palace.

36. Fig. 1. Nobleman's mansion of the Fujiwara age in Shinden style.

    Fig. 2. Plan of Shinden style mansion.

37. Fig. 1. Plan of the Kanin palace.

    Fig. 2. Plan of Shinden style mansion.

38. Streets in the capital of Heian.

39. Phoenix Hall (Hōō-do) of the Byōdōin at Uji. Plan, triple bracketing, hand-rail and pendant of gable.
40. Hall of the Fukiji temple in Bungo, Kyushu. Elevation and section.
41. The Hakushi Amida-do, Uchigo village, Iwaki district, Fukushima province. Elevation and section. Built in 1160.
42. Reconstruction of the city of Hiraizumi after Sato.
43. The Konjikido of the Chusonji.
44. Five-story pagoda of the Daigōji, showing breadths and heights of roofs.
45. Five-story pagoda of the Daigōji with geometrical proportions, after the diagram of Professor Amanuma.
46. The Hachiman shrine at Usa, and the Hiyoshi shrine at Hieizan.
47. The Kamo shrine, Kyoto, side and front views. Rebuilt in 1863. Edo period.
48. Professor Amanuma's restoration of the Yugi pagoda of Mount Koya.
49. Kamakura, with Shogun's mansion inset, after Sato.
50. Mansion of the governor of the Eastern Provinces (Kanto-Kanryo) at Kamakura in the Muromachi period.
51. A birth. Showing interior of a mansion, Kamakura period.
52. The Shōin of a monastery.
53. Fig. 1. Wall and gate with guard-house over it, in military residence of Kamakura period.
    Fig. 2. Bell-tower of the Tōdaiji, Nara, side view elevation and section, front view half-section.
54. The three-story pagoda of the Kōfukuji, Nara. Early Kamakura style.
55. Stupa-shaped pagoda of Ishiyarna temple. Built by Minamoto Yoritomo.
56. The Nandaimon of the Tōdaiji.
57. Details of the Kanshinji.
58. The Shariden, of the Engakuji, Kamakura.
59. Fig. 1. Renge gate of the Toji Temple, Kyoto.
    Fig. 2. Details of roof construction of the Kamakura period. Kozanji temple, Chofu, Yamaguchi prefecture.
60. The Sutra library (Kyōzō) at Kami Daigo temple.
61. Fig. 1. Kanshinji temple, side view.
    Fig. 2. The Kaisando or Founder's Hall of the Eihōji, Toyooka village, Gefu prefecture (Kamakura period).
62. The octagonal pagoda of the Anrakuji temple at Bessho village, Chiisagata district, province of Nagano.
63. The Great Pagoda (Daito) of Negoro temple. Elevation and section.
64. Ginkakuji, Kyoto. Front view and side view.
65. Details of the Kinkakuji.

66. Fig. 1. Side view of the Ki-bitsu shrine, Ichinomiya, Okayama prefecture, built in 1390. Figs 1 to 10. Decorated beam-ends from the bell-tower of the Tōdaiji, Nara.
67. Fig, 1. Oshi-ita.
     FIG. 2. Early form of *shōji*, called Konmeichi *shōji*.
68. Plan of Azuchi castle and surroundings.
69. Fig. 1. Plans of Osaka castle.
     Fig. 2. Old sketch of fortified field headquarters about 1600.
     Fig. 3. Rampart of Osaka castle.
     Fig. 4. Gate of the castle of Sakura.
     Fig. 5. Castle Gate (Masugata).
70. Osaka castle as defended by Hideyori in 1614.
71. Fig. 1. Kitchen and refectory of the Myōhōin Kyoto; side view and front view.
     Fig. 2. The eight-fold roof of the Momoyama period.
72. Dai-butsu-den or Hall of the Great Buddha of the Tōdaiji, Nara.
73. Fig. 1. The Great Buddha temple of the Hōkōji, from a picture of 1794.
     Fig. 2. The Hiunkaku of the Nishi Hongwanji from the western side.
74. The Kokakudai bathroom of the Hiunkaku.
75. The Hiunkaku villa.
76. Jinya or official residence of a smaller feudal lord or local official.
77. The castle and town of Fukuoka, built and laid out by Kuroda Josui and his son Nagamasa after 1600.
78. Plan of the Hon Maru of the Castle of Fukuoka.
79. Plan of the castle town of Matsue.
80. Fig. 1. Plan of the Hon Mara of Okayama castle.
     Fig. 2. The mansion of the Hon Maru of Okayama castle in the time of Ikeda Mitsurnasa, 1632-1672.
81. Plan of the castle town of Okayama.
82. Fig. 1. Plan of the moated castle town of Okayama, Bizen.
     Fig. 2. Plan of the Clan College (Han Gakko) at Okayama.
83. Plan of the castle town of Takada in Echigo.
84. Plan of the city Nagasaki.
85. Fig. 1. Keep of the castle of Nagoya.
     Fig. 2. Keep of Matsue (1600).
86. Fig. 1. Keep of Okayama castle (1597).
     Fig. 2. Keep of Inuyama castle (1600)
     Fig. 3. Keep of Kumamoto castle (1596).
     Fig. 4. Keep of the castle of Matsumoto in Shinano (1590).

87. Fig. 1. The original keep of Edo castle.
   Fig. 2. Flanking guardhouse at entrance of Edo castle.
88. Village of craftsmen laid out by Honami Kōetsu at Takagamine.
89. General plan of Edo castle.
90. Edo castle. O Omote or Outer Palace of the Hon Maru.
91. Edo castle. O Oku or Inner Palace of the Hon Maru, plan 1.
92. Edo castle. O Oku or Inner Palace of the Hon Maru, plan 2.
93. Plan of the mansion of a court noble.
94. Gates of Daimyos' mansions in Edo.
95. Fig. 1. Plan of the. Tōshōgu shrine at Nikko.
   Fig. 2. Plan of Nijo castle.
96. Upper section of the five-storied pagoda at Nikko.
97. Lower section of the five-storied pagoda at Nikko.
98. Plan of the Zen temple of Myōshinji, and plan of its kitchen and refectory.
99. Plan of Zen temple of Manpukuji.
100. Imperial Palace, Kyoto. Koka gate and Seiryōden.
101. Imperial Palace, Kyoto. Front gate and Shishinden.
102. The Imperial Palace shrine or Kashiko-dokoro.
103. Fig. 1. Front of a theatrer.
   Fig. 2. The theater quarter of Saru-waka-cho.
104. Plan of the Yoshiwara pleasure quarter in Edo.
105. Fig. 1. Side street in Edo with guard-house and gates for closing the thoroughfare.
   Fig. 2. Fireman's watch-tower.
   Fig. 3. Fireproof storehouse.
106. Fig. 1. Plan of public bath house at Osaka.
   Fig. 2. Plan of public bath house in Edo.
   Fig. 3. Bath tub with gabled porch in public bath house.
107. Bathroom interior.
108. Fig. 1. Large farmhouse in Tsutsuki village, Kyoto.
   Fig. 2. Narrow residence characteristic of Kyoto, known as "eel housing."
109. Korean peasant's house built of logs and mud.
110. Kachu-yashiki or Samurai residence at Kita-bori, Matsue.
111. Fig. 1. Plan of the residence of a Samurai of middle class.
   Fig. 2. Street front and gatehouse of the above.
112. A Benie print-seller.
113. Fig. 1. Privy of an inn at the end of a short covered way at right angles to a veranda.
   Fig. 2. The interior of above, with ventilation window.

114. Tiles.

115. Roof shapes.

116. Lattice windows.

117. Staircases.

118. Ceilings.

119. Wooden lanterns.

120. Hot spring bath houses.

121. Fig. 1. The simple staircase of an inn.
Fig. 2. A renaissance cupola added to a hot spring bathing hotel in pure Japanese style.

122. Plan and elevation of a modern house in Japanese style.

123. Section of an ordinary Japanese house to show construction.

FOREWORD

Arthur Lindsay Sadler was born in London in 1882. He studied
Oriental languages at Oxford University, graduating with a Bachelor
of Arts degree in 1908 and a Master of Arts degree in 1911. Although
his studies focused on the Hebrew and Assyrian languages, Sadler
moved to Japan in 1909, citing the influence of his teacher, Oxford
university professor Dr. C. J. Ball, and Edward Morse's descriptions of
Japanese houses and gardens in his 1886 book, *Japanese Homes and
their Surroundings*, one of the first books on the topic published in the
English language. Sadler taught English and Latin at Dairoku Kōto
Gakko (the Number Six Higher Secondary School) in Okayama for
nine years before moving to Tokyo in 1918 to teach English at Peer's
College (now Gakushu-in University). In 1922 he took a position as
Professor of Oriental Studies at the University of Sydney, where he
taught until his retirement in 1948. From 1931-37 Sadler also served as
a professor of Japanese at the Royal Military College in Sydney. Upon
retiring, he returned to England, where he stayed until his death in 1970.[1]
Sadler was a prolific writer and translator, as well as a teacher.
Following his move to Australia, he began almost two decades of
writing and translating, covering many different aspects of Japanese
culture, including literature, traditional drama, flower arrangement,
tea ceremony, samurai tenets, architecture, and the influence of
Japanese culture on other countries, as well as history and historical
biography. Sadler considered himself to be a student of history,[2] and
it is obvious from his many publications that he was an avid student
of Japan's culture and aesthetics as well. He was quite knowledgeable
about the many subjects of his books, using his historian's mind to
piece together the various elements of the political and social contexts
that gave rise to certain cultural activities.

Sadler looked at Japan's culture and aesthetics not only from a
historian's standpoint, however, as he also viewed Japan with the
eyes of an outsider and endeavored to introduce Japanese culture
to a Western (specifically English-speaking) audience. Sadler often
used comparisons between Japan and Europe as a means to clarify

specific cultural differences. The introductions to his translations of historic works of literature and drama include informative descriptions of the history and the then-contemporary state of the arts. For example, in *Japanese Plays: Noh-Kyogen-Kabuki* (1934), Sadler explains how Noh drama is regarded by the people of Japan and its relationship to Japanese culture, as well as makes comparisons to opera and Greek theater.[3]

In one of his early books, the 1928 *The Ten Foot Square Hut and Tales of the Heike*, his translations of the *Hōjiki* and the *Heiki Monogatari*, Sadler notes of the texts, "both of them masterpieces of Japanese literature of the thirteenth century, and dealing with the same period from a different point of view."[4] Sadler's ability to illuminate the various differing points of view at any one time in Japan's history or the many variations within a single aesthetic pursuit is a hallmark of his research and writing. In his 1933 *The Art of Flower Arrangement in Japan*, Sadler discusses "the history and principal varieties of the Way of Flowers," including close to 150 illustrations of examples of arrangements from four major schools of flower arrangement. In *Cha-no-yu: The Japanese Tea Ceremony* (1933), Sadler includes short essays describing the important roles of almost 100 tea masters in the development of the tea ceremony, noting that "these men are the esthetic ancestors of the nation."[5] In *Japanese Plays*, Sadler endeavored to include plays that were representative of each of the three traditional styles, giving the reader an easy way to compare and contrast the different styles of theater.

Sadler well understood the role of aesthetics in the cultural and political history of Japan and focused much of his research to emphasize that integral relationship and the major historical figures who were involved in shaping Japan's history and culture. In his biographic account *The Maker of Modern Japan: The Life of Shogun Tokugawa Ieyasu* (1937), Sadler emphasizes Ieyasu's historic role, "it was he who made the system under which Japan as we know it was forged into shape."[6] It was under that system that many of the arts flourished, and Sadler writes in *Cha-no-yu*, "it was the strong and centralized administration of the Tokugawa Shoguns that made the esthetic control of the Empire possible and easy...Indeed Cha-no-yu may be considered an epitome of Japanese civilization."[7] He continues, "some knowledge of Cha-no-yu is evidently necessary to an understanding of the development of the nation, its ideas and its taste... Cha-no-yu, like Noh and similar institutions, continues to flourish more vigorously than ever. Should it cease to do so the soul of Japan will have departed from her, and that is hardly thinkable."[8]

Although he made a point of describing himself as a "layman in architectural matters"[9] in *A Short History of Japanese Architecture*, retitled for this edition *Japanese Architecture: A Short History*, and in other books he writes that his work "may be considered as an attempt to supply further information"[10] and "not to give instruction"[11] in a particular art, Sadler's understanding of the traditional arts of Japan was extensive. He wrote as teacher and interpreter of Japanese history and culture, endeavoring to fill in the voids of information available in the English language for anyone interested in studying Japan. "Material of this kind is necessary for the study of Japanese culture as prescribed in this university and is not available in any reliable form that can be recommended to students, except perhaps in the work of [Josiah] Conder, which is, unfortunately, unobtainable."[12] Yet he understood that his mid-twentieth century audience mostly was not well-informed about Japan, and he wrote in a style that was accessible to those who knew little of Japan as well as those who were avid students of the country and culture.

Sadler lamented the lack of information on Japan in general (and accurate information in particular), since few people could read original Japanese texts, as could he. In his introduction to *The Maker of Modern Japan*, he writes, "Possibly lack of material available in European languages, leading to the very free use of the imagination, is the partial cause of the great want of accuracy in statements concerning Japanese history in many books that treat of it..."[13] Considering his potential audience, he continues, "This book is not peppered with references, for they would be quite useless except to those who read Japanese historical texts, and for them the list of sources at the end will, I think, be sufficient."[14]

For each of his books, Sadler drew from a variety of sources. A quick review of his bibliography for *A Short History of Japanese Architecture* shows that he reviewed Japanese texts dealing with much more than just architecture. He also cites sources in Japanese customs, Buddhist art, Japanese history, and historical biography. As would be expected, his reference list for non-Japanese language books includes publications on Japanese art, architecture, and gardens. Sadler added annotation for each non-Japanese language book cited, noting the ease of reading and the amount and quality of the information. It is interesting to note that most of these books were published in the years 1935-37, demonstrating, perhaps, a growing interest in Japanese architecture in Western countries, as well as Sadler's own interest in keeping up with the latest research in Japanese architecture.

For Sadler, architecture, like flower arrangement, traditional theater, and the way of tea, was a window into Japanese culture and history. As the socio-political situation in Japan changed, so too did the architectural style favored by the elite classes. Sadler notes, "Countries write their history very legibly in the things they build and the way they treat the face of the earth, and the Japanese have done it as clearly as any."[15] In his preface to *A Short History of Japanese Architecture*, Sadler straightforwardly states the objective of the book: to provide "direct visual means of giving some insight into the phases through which Japanese culture has passed and the elements of which it is composed."[16]

It is clear from his earlier works that Sadler was interested in the insight into the history of the country that traditional Japanese architecture provided him. He often included detailed descriptions of buildings and gardens as background information to give a broad understanding of a traditional art or place. For example, in *Japanese Plays* he includes a sketch of a theater, as well as detailed written descriptions of Noh and Kabuki theaters (including a comparison to European theaters), emphasizing the relationship of the various architectural elements of the theaters to the different audience seating areas, reflecting the diverse social strata of audience members.[17] In his research, Sadler was very careful to note the differences between the lifestyle of the elite social classes and that of commoners. In *A Short History of Japanese Architecture*, although the emphasis is on major public buildings (primarily temples and shrines) and aristocratic residences, Sadler also discusses the houses of the common people and compares them to those of the elite.

True to his historian background, Sadler organized *A Short History of Japanese Architecture* with the first section consisting of chapters describing the development of Japanese architecture over different time periods, starting from 660 BCE and ending at 1860 CE. Each chapter begins with a brief description of the politics of that specific era, and Sadler then places the architecture of that time within the political context. He includes detailed descriptions of important buildings, emphasizing their identifying and/or unusual characteristics, and highlights any extant buildings from each time period. While it is obvious that the text was carefully researched, it is not without its inaccuracies, both historical (such as Sadler's statement that the shrine at Ise is re-built every 25 years—it is rebuilt every 20 years) and linguistic (for example, Sadler consistently writes *shōin* incorrectly—which alters its meaning; it should be *shoin*). Still, the text is full of detail, very readable, and offers a variety of information that typically is not included in books on architectural history for a general audience.

After the chronological history, Sadler includes several chapters that are illustrative of buildings in specific time periods, including descriptions of certain architectural elements and rooms (sliding partitions, ceilings, toilets, baths, and kitchens) that differ greatly from those in the West, as well as the role of "the architect" in traditional buildings. These chapters give insight into traditional life in Japan and are especially useful to readers who know little about Japanese architecture and culture. This section is followed by an unusual but quite interesting set of appendices. The first is the list of illustrations from a book of Japanese architecture, which Sadler provides as a "comprehensive list of historic Japanese buildings according to their successive epochs."[18] The second is a "Comparative Table of Dates," a chart of parallel timelines of political eras in India, China, Korea, and Japan. The third appendix is a "Glossary of Architectural Terms," which includes the *kanji*, or ideographs, for each word as well as the Romanized spelling and a short definition in English.

The appendices are an atypical inclusion in a book that does not intend to be comprehensive but purports to give a "short" account of the history; nonetheless they are quite useful for the student of Japanese architecture. They are not without discrepancy, however. Sadler's "Comparative Table of Dates," along with the years he lists for the historical periods in each chapter (e.g. Momoyama 1570-1616; Edo 1616-1860, etc.), do not match those typically used by other scholars (even others writing about Japanese architecture at same time as Sadler, such as Kishida Hideto in *Japanese Architecture* (1936), which Sadler lists as a reference).

Following the appendices is the second part of the book—almost half the total pages, filled with illustrated plates, each with a brief caption. Although the plates are an interesting combination of quick hand sketches and hardline drawings, the inconsistencies in line weight and style are a bit distracting (but give the book a feeling of being hand-made). Having all the plates at the end of the text allows for easy comparison between them but is less convenient when reading, especially since so few of the illustrations are referenced directly in the body of the text (and some, such as the "forms of ancient houses" are not discussed at all). However, many of the images include a great amount of detail that again is unusual in a "short history" and useful to the student of Japanese architecture. The plans of different castle complexes, for example, have rooms shown and labeled, which allows for straightforward comparing and contrasting.

Another unusual aspect of this particular text on Japanese archi-tecture, which again is true to Sadler's historian background, is that the author takes the reader back to the very roots of much of the architecture that made its way across Asia to Japan—all the way back to India. Many historians discuss the Indian stupa as the predeces-sor to the pagoda in China and hence in Japan, but few include the relationship of Buddhist temples in India to those in China. Fewer still bring up India when discussing the Japanese tea ceremony room, but Sadler finds a connection even there. "The fixing of the size of the Tea-room as four and a half mats, the size of Chomei's hut [Kamo-no-Chōmei, who was disappointed "at not being allowed to succeed to the ancestral position of Lord Warden of the Shrine of Kamo in Kyoto that caused him to forsake the world and go live in the hills"[19]], indicates its descent from the cell of the Buddhist recluse Vimalakirrti who miraculously entertained in it the Buddha and three thousand five hundred of his saints and disciples."[20]

One important aspect of Japanese architecture that is missing in this book is a section on *sukiya*-style architecture, the style favored for tearooms and many aristocratic residences of the Momoyama and Edo periods (1573-1867 CE). Sadler notes only that he discusses the tea ceremony room in detail in his earlier book, *Cha-no-yu*, in which he calls the tearoom (despite the initial influence of outside cultures) "entirely Japanese"[21]—a label he gives to no other architecture in Japan. The lack of discussion of the *sukiya* style is also intriguing, given the time period in which Sadler was writing. By the 1920s, young Japanese architects were very interested in designing in the style that had become popular in Europe, the Modern style, and were looking at *sukiya* architecture as the root of Japanese Modernism. Western architects, such as the German Modernist Bruno Taut, visited Japan and gave credence to the Japanese Modernists by "identifying Katsura as *the* masterpiece of functionalist architecture."[22] Sadler directly addresses this issue in *Cha-no-yu*: "This movement may be called Modern only in Europe, for it appears to a great extent to be, where it is not influenced by machinery of some kind, a copying of the national outlook and taste of Japan in these spheres, for though it may only lately have dawned on continental artists and decorators that a house is a machine to live in and from which all superfluous and irritating ornaments should be banished, the contact between this part of Europe and Japan has been too close of late to allow of the discovery being entirely an independent one. The necessity for strict economy in life and the lack of means for ostentation which post-war conditions have brought about, combined with the impulse to simplicity inspired by militarism, may supply the reason for the departure from previous standards."[23]

Referring to the great tea master and *sukiya* tearoom designer Sen no Rikyu, Sadler writes that Modernism "might not be unsuitably described as the Rikyu style, for Sen Rikyu perhaps did more than any other artist to stimulate and standardize that sort of architecture."[24] However, he observes that others may think of Modernism as having ancient European roots, but notes in quoting Pericles "that his countrymen 'loved beauty with economy and culture without softness,' there may be pointed out the strange truth that Japan has preserved this spirit up to the present time…"[25] Sadler elaborates in *Japanese Plays*: "They [the Japanese] have always realized, and tried to avoid, the monotony of life by studying it as an art and by cultivating the asymmetric and the suggestive. And yet owing to their practical appreciation of economy and dislike of the superfluous, they have for centuries practised standardization, and these qualities are to be seen very clearly marked in their dramatic forms, in the uniform structure of the pieces and their variety of detail."[26]

He just as easily could have been writing about *sukiya*-style architecture.

Sadler emphasizes that the "disciplined estheticism" found in Japan and not in other countries is due in part to "Teaism" as refined by Rikyu (along with the "antiquity of the civilization" of Japan).[27]

Lack of taste and balance in decoration, a confused ostentation and want of any system of etiquette permeating all classes of society have been and still are very noticeable in the West and America, and practically all visitors to Japan seem to be struck by the strange phenomenon that good manners are as natural to the peasant and workman as to the leisured classes.[28]

He continues, "…and it was the strong and centralized administration of the Tokugawa Shoguns that made the aesthetic control of the Empire possible and easy."[29]

Many architectural historians have discussed the aesthetic control of the Tokugawa shogunate and noted its influence on the development of the *sukiya* style, seeing *sukiya* architecture as true Japanese architecture and highlighting the Katsura Imperial Villa in Kyoto as the epitome of the style. For German architect Bruno Taut, for example, "the Katsura Palace is a completely isolated miracle in the civilized world."[30] Sadler, on the other hand, mentions Katsura only twice, once with a brief description: "a very simple set of thatched roof buildings…the villa has infinite variety in its construction and all the details are uncommon. Naturally it is much imbued with the Chanoyu feeling."[31] The other mention is in an endnote, Sadler's response to Taut's belief that "Japan's architectural arts could not rise higher than Katsura, nor sink lower than Nikkō [the highly ornate Nikkō Tōshōgū mausoleum for Tokugawa Ieyasu]."[32]

Sadler's note regarding Taut's comments shows that he was aware of the argument of Nikkō versus Katsura as the essence of Japanese taste, yet he declines to discuss it directly. Instead Sadler asserts, "The best known works of the Edo period are undoubtedly the shrines at Nikko."[33] In *The Maker of Modern Japan*, he describes the Nikkō complex as "that perfectly situated and gorgeous mausoleum…And with it, too, commenced a new style of architecture to be perpetrated in the hardly less resplendent shrines of his successors…"[34] Whereas Sadler sees the mausoleum buildings as "a new architectural style," most architectural historians of the day focused more on their exaggerated detail and other "defects" that prohibited them from representing "the pure 'spirit of Japan.'"[35] In *Japanese Architecture* Kishida Hideto states, "The Daijingu shrines of Ise and this detached palace at Katsura are the two greatest masterpieces of Japanese architecture. To see Ise and Katsura is to see Japan and its architecture. Compare Katsura and Nikkō, then you can distinguish clearly what is pure Japanese and what is not. This comparison is so striking that it offers the student of Japanese architecture an ideal contrast."[36]

Although Sadler typically pointed out contrasting ideas in his publications, in *A Short History of Japanese Architecture* he chose not to involve himself in the debates around Modernism and "pure" Japanese architecture. Perhaps his feeling of the distinct suitability of the Nikkō Tōshōgū mausoleum as an appropriate celebration of Tokugawa Ieyasu's life and death, based on his deep knowledge of and respect for the shogun, as is apparent in his biography of Ieyasu, *The Maker of Modern Japan*, made the debate seem irrelevant. For Sadler, the 17th century Nikkō Tōshōgū was the finest example of the last new architectural style in Japan, and thus he chose to focus the final chapter of his history of Japanese architecture on it, noting that thereafter "things went on without much change till about 1700, when a great deterioration set in," and "gradually everything became stereotyped and conventional."[37]

There is nothing stereotyped and conventional about this book, however, as Sadler leads the reader through the epochs of changing architectural forms and socio-political circumstances, packing an enormous amount of detail and intrigue into his "short account" of the history of Japanese architecture.

MIRA LOCHER
August 13, 2008

PREFACE

IT was probably an attraction to Japanese buildings and gardens, first acquired from a perusal of Morse's *Japanese Homes and their Surroundings* in the Bodleian Library many years ago, as much as the historical interest or the wise counsel of that very eminent orientalist Dr. C. J. Ball, that decided me to go to Japan rather than to the Near East, which was then the more obvious region for research. And these houses and gardens were certainly no disappointment, but a source of continual pleasure all the time I stayed there—a diversion I regret I have missed since leaving Japan, for Australia is in these things the diametric opposite to that country as it is in most others.

And though a layman in architectural matters, with only a claim to some appreciation of them as a student of history, I have lived for some ten years or so in three old Japanese houses in an ancient castle town, as well as built a new one. Perhaps there may, in this, be an application of the Japanese proverb which states that the acolyte before the temple gate repeats the scriptures he has not learned, or, as one adroit translator puts it, "The saint's maid quotes Latin." More-over, fortunate residence in a comely old English town and six years of leisure in one of the most elegant of Oxford colleges, both in buildings and garden, were a natural education in what is shapely and harmonious in various types of Western architecture. So it has been an entertaining task after many days to epithet these drawings and plans from the books I happen to have read, and put them together in some sort of chronological order in the hope that they may be a direct visual means of giving some insight into the phases through which Japanese culture has passed and the elements of which it is composed.

A. L. SADLER. *Sydney, July,* 1941

CHAPTER 1

Introduction

THE purpose of this work is to give a short account of the growth of Japanese architecture and its connexion with the history and culture of the people. Countries write their history very legibly in the things they build and the way they treat the face of the earth, and the Japanese have done it as clearly as any. The character of the land with its abundance of timber and the natural taste of the inhabitants for this medium have combined to present us with the most advanced wooden architecture in the world; and the isolation of Japan, on the one hand, and its relations with the continent, on the other, have preserved in these islands specimens of architecture that do not survive in the countries of their origin.

The earliest buildings of Japan are the simple rectilinear structures of the primitive dwelling houses which survive only in a somewhat modified form in the Shinto shrines, and seem to be of the same type as those found in the islands of the Pacific. And residences have continued to be predominantly of this type, for it seems to suit the temperament of the people. The severe winter cold prevalent in most parts of the Japanese islands has not caused much modification in what is essentially a sub-tropical style, or even brought about the introduction of any heating system like those found in Korea and China. Simplicity has been preferred to warmth, and the cold kept at bay to a certain extent by braziers and padded garments. But these houses are no more than simple construction, and architecture, properly speaking, entered Japan with Buddhism in the sixth century. The origin of both the philosophy and the architecture was India and they were only modified in passing through China and Korea. From the stone reliefs of the post-Asoka period at Sanchi and elsewhere it is evident that the early Indian buildings were also of wood,[38] for even after they were rendered in stone they retained all the characteristics of their original construction. But in India stone and brick entirely superseded this wooden style and even in

China these materials were largely used for temples, bridges, gates, and pagodas. In Japan this architecture assumed its original wooden form and did not depart from it, for (with the exception of the stylobates, foundation stones, castle ramparts, and facings of moats and gates in and after the sixteenth century) nothing but Buddhist statuary, garden ornaments, and tombstones has ever been made of anything but wood.

The introduction of this Indian style into Japan was not unlike that of classical architecture into England, though there is less variation in it than there is between Romanesque, the different types of Gothic, and the later Renaissance styles. The principal difference is in the details of the pillars and bracketing and the slope of the roofs. It never affected residences to the same extent either, for the most elaborate mansions in Japan were quite unlike temples. They merely borrowed a little bracketing here and there, and some patterns on the roof tiles. Castles came later, and were not much used as residences; we do not find any such mannered institutions as Hatfield, Blenheim, or Castle Howard, nor anything like the odd Gothic fancies of Pugin, though some comparison might perhaps be made between Knole and the residential part of Edo Castle.

The Japanese love of nature made them disinclined to shut themselves up in a kind of big storehouse even though the winds might blow. That sort of building they reserved for their possessions; and their residences, whether military, civil, or ecclesiastical, were never much more than structures just stout enough to keep off the weather, particularly the sun and rain, and especially designed as shelters from which to view the garden or a distant landscape. It is for this latter purpose as a rule that a room is added in the roof; for, with the exception of shops and inns and restaurants and some houses in big cities, most Japanese houses are single-storied, though that does not mean that they are necessarily lacking in height. Important buildings such as palaces, temples, and mansions, and even the houses of large landowners, have very lofty roofs quite high enough to contain several stories, and temples that have a double roof with two sets of eaves one over the other do not use the space in the upper one.

On the whole Japanese buildings give the impression of being planned from within outwards, for use and not to be looked at from outside. As they are so often secluded behind a courtyard the gate is apt to be the most noticeable feature, and, since by its shape it denoted the rank of its owner, it was at times of a somewhat elaborate nature. The great gates of the Imperial Palace, the four-legged gate of the Court noble, and the threefold or storied gate of the temple are all significant, and it was not perhaps so strange that in later days the gates of the mansions of the feudal nobility should be regulated by the government according to their owners' incomes.

It is probably well known that one of the ancient titles of the Emperor, *Mikado* means "August Gate," but it may not be generally realized how very architectural are most titles in Japan. The expression translated "His Majesty" *(Heika)* means "below the steps" (of the palace), and that translated "Highness" *(Denka),* "below the mansion." *Tono* (mansion) still means "nobleman," while another medieval word *yakata,* with the same significance, is now obsolete. *In* (temple) was the word for a retired Emperor or a dead Shogun. *Mon-in* (Dowager Empress) means the "Retired One of the palace gate." *Kamon* (House Gate) means "descendants of the House," i.e. the Tokugawa family, while the word for lineage itself, *mombatsu,* means "one whose gate is meritorious," and *meimon* (gate of repute) means "a noble family." *Tsubone* (the title of a lady-in-waiting) means "courtyard," and the wives of nobles and Shoguns were called *kita-no-kata* (the lady of the north or inner side of the house), or *mi-daidokoro* (august kitchen), with the same meaning. The terms still in use for a lady, *okusama* or *go reikei*[39] mean respectively "inner apartment" and "'august bed-chamber." We have, too, *go bō* (honorable cell) for a monk, and *o heya sama* (honorable chamber) for a noble's concubine. Similar, too, is the use of such words as *-sai* (study) and *-an* (cottage) for the terminations of the literary names of scholars and aesthetes and retired people.

The material of Japanese buildings is almost exclusively wood with the exception of the pottery of the tiles. All joints are mortised, tenoned, and pegged, and the gutters are of wood or bamboo.

Until recently there were only bamboo pipes, and water was drawn from a well with wooden buckets and a pulley of porcelain. No nails were used anywhere and the only things likely to be of metal would be the pushes of the sliding doors, and the iron shutters of the windows of the fireproof storehouse if there was one. It is not perhaps surprising that in the technique of wood-working Japanese surpass other nations, for construction is nowhere hidden and the surface of the material is left plain without paint both within and without—the only exception being the lacquering of some details, the preparation for which requires a very exacting standard of cabinet work.

Since Japan has always been autocratically governed and the people have never had any say in the administration, buildings like parliament houses or town or moot halls are conspicuous by their absence until modern times. In fact, places of assembly of any kind except bath houses and theaters are rare, for gatherings of people were not regarded with any favour by the government, and where they existed were always supervised and inspected by it. Even law courts were not very noticeable, because the commissioners for justice, who were both judicial and administrative, dispensed this commodity in their own mansions and in their own fashion. And this fashion did not run so much to prisons and dungeons as did some others, for though the former did exist, the custom of prescribing such penalties as did not require any building, and confining handcuffed in their own houses people who seemed to require such restraint, resulted in very considerable economy. The Shogun, for instance, did not need such a building as the Tower to confine an objectionable nobleman, but ordered him under arrest in the mansion of another baron. If anything further were needed he would be exiled at his own expense or ordered to commit suicide on his own mats.

Buddhist temples, again, are chiefly colleges or monasteries or both, and the congregational element is not prominent in them, while in Shinto shrines it is not present at all, for worship is purely individual and sporadic. As time went on, places of assembly were more and more restricted, till in the Tokugawa era the only places where people could congregate were theaters and pleasure quarters, both supervised, and prohibited for the governing class.

The Japanese residence, being but a succession of rooms without walls and only divided by sliding doors, does not admit of much privacy—a fact that must have had considerable influence on the manners of its inhabitants; for without suitable etiquette and uncommon neatness it would not be tolerable to live in. And it is likely that the comparative abstinence of the Japanese woman from romantic adventures is to no small extent due to her life in a house that is little more than one large room open at any time to a *coup d'oeil* from one end to the other. What chance, asks E. V. Lucas, has cupid in Holland where there are no groves? Much less chance has he in the Japanese house where there are not even walls to have ears. This does not apply so much to the men, whose inclinations in this direction are catered for in many-storied pavilions.

Fire and earthquake have doubtless helped to keep Japanese architecture what it is, for a building out of which the inmates can step at once from any part is convenient for both, while the construction even of quite lofty pagodas has proved fairly stable in the latter.

Fully as important as the building of palace, mansion, temple, or residence, if not more so, is the garden, the treatment of the space that surrounds them. Though this is entirely a separate subject it has the closest connexion with architecture, because the garden is usually planned with the buildings, which are arranged about it with a courtyard or semi-courtyard effect, or with detached parts joined by covered ways or bridges. So the garden is not so much an adjunct to the house as an essential part of it, to be designed by an expert together with it or before it. This is why there is greater variety in the houses than might be considered probable when the construction is as standardized as it is, for all rooms have long been multiples of a *tatami* or floor-mat[40] (6 x 3 feet) and all sliding doors are the same height and width (3.8 by 3 feet) with a fixed size for the pillars according to the scale of the building. All of which makes for economy and rapidity of construction.

It will be noted, however, that, though the Japanese house seems for some centuries to have been very unlike that of any Western country, as it is traced farther back it becomes less so. The characteristic mats disappear from the floors, and the ceiling from the roof, while small windows[41] take the place of the papered *shōji,* for sliding doors were yet unknown. The thatched roof and earthen floor make it a peasant's hut such as must have been fairly universal in those times. The changes took place in the big cities, where the best artisans and architect-artificers competed for the favour of Shogun or feudal lord—in the Imperial Capital of Kyoto, or the military capitals of Kamakura or Edo, or the great commercial centres like Osaka, Sakai, or Nagasaki. But in the remote country conditions do not change much, and the country of Japan is still very isolated between ranges of hills and narrow winding valleys or small islands where even now few but country folk go. So there may still be seen survivals from the pretatami era, dwellings lived in as they have been from the earliest times. And what there is beyond this shows very clearly how the Indian culture, together with sculpture and painting influenced by the Greek colonies of Gandhara, came across by way of China and Korea, sometimes indirectly through the latter country, and in later times more directly from China. For Japan has never been slow in adopting advantages from a dominant country and in showing less enthusiasm for a decadent one.

Japanese architecture is described as a branch of Chinese, but little of the Chinese is indigenous. China is somewhat to Japan as Rome is to England, but behind China lay India, the equivalent of Greece. And India in her turn is perhaps indebted to Persia and Babylonia, as is Greece to Crete and Egypt. Much, therefore, of this Japanese culture may be of Aryan origin, for the influence of Buddhist and Hindu thought shaped the Japanese mind in the same way as Semitic monotheism did that of Europe.

> The bell of the Jetavana Vihara
> Tolls the knell of the impermanence of phenomena.[42]

But in spite of the Japanese conviction of the impermanence of things, it is remarkable what a large number of interesting and ancient buildings are still to be seen in the country. From the famous Hōryuji monastery of the seventh century right on, these massive wooden structures reveal the characteristics of the various dynasties of China as well as the original inspiration from India. It is no longer possible to see these things in China, for there disintegration and destruction have been fatal to the past; like other continental lands, it has been subject to rough invaders whom not even the "ten thousand mile long castle" could keep out. Destruction there has been, too, in Japan, and what remains is but a small part of what once was; but in spite of the damage caused by fires and civil wars there has been a great deal of intelligent rebuilding and restoration, which still continues—as witness the recent recreation of the great keep of Hideyoshi's castle by the city of Osaka exactly as it was, but in steel and concrete. Great hotels and theaters are also being built in this Momoyama style, and even Christian churches are being put up in Japanese style as they were in the sixteenth century, instead of in suburban Gothic as they were formerly in the Meiji era.

Moreover (and I am, of course, indebted to them for everything in this book) there is a large number of eminent professors and scholars in Japan who have investigated and compared and catalogued and repaired their masterpieces of architecture, and published admirable works illustrated by fine photographs that supply a mass of information about them. Professors Ito, Sekino, Kida, Amanuma, and Fujita are among the most outstanding of these, and this book is no more than a resume of what they have written. With a view to increasing its usefulness for those who wish to examine really good and detailed photographs of the structures mentioned, I have added references to Professor Amanuma's great work, *A Pictorial Record of the History of Japanese Architecture (Nippon Kenchikushi Zuroku),* indispensable to any really interested in the subject, consisting of a series of illustrations of all the important buildings, accompanied by comments in Japanese. Though the comment may not be understandable the pictures speak for themselves.

CHAPTER 2

Early Period (660 B.C.–A.D. 540)

Though no specimens of the most ancient Japanese buildings have survived, their nature can to a large extent be conjectured from descriptions in the ancient writings such as the *Kōjiki* and the *Nihongi,* from pictures and models found in the dolmen tombs, and from the Shinto shrines which conservative sentiment has preserved little changed from the earliest times. It is written that in the days of the Emperor Suinin, who succeeded in 29 B.C., the sacred mirror and regalia were removed from the palace where they had been hitherto, and this act marked the separation of residence and shrine. The shrine, which is that of Ise, was evidently built just like the residence and has not since been altered. The regulation that it should be rebuilt every twenty-five years, i.e., every generation, is no doubt a survival of the custom of moving to a new palace on the death of an Emperor, since birth and death are the greatest pollutions. Parturition houses are spoken of in the ancient texts and are even now still found in some parts of the country.

In the details of its construction the Ise shrine is the earliest type, for its roof is perfectly straight and it is built in the simplest manner without any ornament. The rafters project in the form of a crotch above the roof and the ridge lies in the angle of these crotches, while on that again are short logs to hold it in place. Originally its timbers were bound together with wistaria withes like those of the palace, but later they came to be secured with peg and mortise.

This type of roof was originally forbidden to all but Imperial Residences and the *Kōjiki* mentions the case of the roof of a noble being pulled down because it was too high.[43] And to this day in Japan the height of the roof is a sign of social standing, as it was in the Tokugawa period when only farmers of some importance in a village were allowed to have anything above the ordinary one, or such elaborations as a hipped gable or a projecting wing.

The models and carvings that have been excavated show a high pitched roof sometimes of the sort called *irimoya* or hipped gable, and several of these houses are raised above the ground on pillars and entered by a ladder like the Ise shrine. All these early dwellings are very definitely of the Polynesian type, from which the Japanese dwelling house has never departed much; it is only after the entry of Buddhism into Japan that temples began to be built in the Chinese, or more correctly, the Indian, style, for such it really is, and after a while this came to affect the shrine and residence. Tiles and bracketed capitals and ornamental windows made their appearance and the line of the roof assumed a curve. On the other hand, the native style in its turn reacted on this Buddhist architecture in restraining the use of color and ornament and maintaining a severe line and wooden construction, as contrasted with the extravagant curves and brick and stone structures favored in China. Though the earlier temples were colored outside as well as in, with some exceptions[44] shrines remained of unpainted timber. But though the Imperial Shrine of Ise has retained so many early characteristics, in one respect that of Izumo, which commemorates the equally ancient rulers of that province who handed over their dominion to the descendants of the Sun Goddess, has perhaps kept an older style in its plan. Unlike Ise which has the entrance in the front *(hira-iri)* Izumo has it in the gable end *(tsumairi)* and the interior is divided into two by a partition extending from the pillar in the center to the side wall. This shrine is thirty-six feet square without its verandas and has a gabled roof. The entrance is on the right-hand side of the center, thus recalling that of the primitive hut, like a tent of brushwood, which Japanese archaeologists postulate as the primitive home of the ordinary people in succession to the dugout which may have been the earliest of all. Thus, should necessity bring Japan back to this condition, as it threatens to do with Europe, it may well be regarded, like conscription, as but a return to the good old times.

This square form is found also in ancient China, and the possibility that there has been some influence from the continent must not be overlooked, in view of the close relations between the Izumo Deities and the mainland. But this shape, too, has always been to a great extent that of the ordinary farm-house in Japan, modified by additions where more room was needed.[45] The space is then divided into four rooms round the central pillar. This pillar (Mi-naka-bashira, the August Central Pillar) seems to be that which Izanami and Izanagi, the Japanese Adam and Eve, are described as perambulating at their marriage ceremony.

Another variety of this type is the Otori shrine, which has two pillars instead of one, with connecting partitions to the side walls, thus forming one room in front of the other, the inner one being used as the sanctuary. The worshippers are here in front of the divine emblem instead of at the side of it as in the Izumo shrine. And when the outer chamber is made about half as large again as the. inner we have the style of the Sumiyoshi shrine. And there is a type of farmhouse corresponding to the Otori style, that known as Kuni-naka-sumai, where the main portion of the building has these two pillars. An example of a house that is apparently a survival of the Izumo plan is that in Amatsu village of Tansei district of the province of Echizen. It is 21 by 36 feet and is divided into two parts, the inner one with a wooden floor covered with matting and the outer with a floor of hard earth. This outer space is called Oi or O Yue, dialetic for O Ie, the House Place. The left side is called the Upper House (O Yue no karni) and the right the Lower House (O Yue no shimo). In the center is the hearth and in the middle of the floored part is the Daikyoku Bashira or Center Pillar. The fact that the lower part is called the House Place suggests that it was the original building with the hearth in its center, and that the inner part was added later. This inner part consists of two rooms, one of ten mats with an alcove and Buddhist shrine, which is the main reception room, and another six-mat chamber beside it called Nando. This Nando is the original of the Chōdai or canopied dais found in the residence of Imperial Personages and Court nobles, and is still so called in the country. Nando means the place where things are put, i.e. clothes, therefore dressing-room and so bedroom. Another name for it is Kakima, which is evidently a corruption of Kage-no-ma (dark room). Behind this there is a three-mat room in which the Buddhist priest is accommodated when he pays a visit, otherwise used as a storeroom. The space of earth by the entrance is where guests are received, and the doorless and usually wall-less *pissoir* outside it is common in farmhouses, and is there for purely practical purposes, for fertilizer is valuable.

Example of the Otori style may be seen in many ancient dwellings to be found in the Iga district, Shiga Prefecture, of which Plate 5 Fig. 1 is one of the simplest. Here the inner part is one foot higher than the outer and the two rooms in it have a ceiling. The outer part is used to receive ordinary guests, and the inner especially favored ones. The sitting-room (*d*) has its floor covered with bran about two inches deep, with straw matting laid over it. This room is called Nyuji, the meaning of which is unknown. It is also called Omote (exterior). The inner rooms (*e*) and (*f*) are called Oku (interior) and have a wood floor. Modern hygiene has brought about the abolition of the bran covering and matting in favor of a board floor, but this is still kept half a foot or so lower than that of the inner room, so that, counting the *tokonoma*, the house has three levels like the Jodan, Chudan, and Gedan in the mansion of a noble. These houses of Iga have mud walls and most of them still have only small lattice windows with neither *shōji* nor *amado*, while inside they have wooden sliding doors instead of *fusuma*. It was not till the Ashikaga age that these were introduced in the capital and later still in the provinces. Till then the Japanese house had none of the charactristics we now associate with it and did not differ much from the European cottage. These people do not reckon the size of the rooms by the number of *tatami* or mats (for they have none, since they belong to the pre-tatami period), but by the number of widths of matting from the edge of the raised floor to the threshold beam. Four of these would be about eight *tatami*, which is the usual size of these rooms.[46]

The influence of these early dwellings is apparent also in the arrangement of the first Buddhist temples, since these were simply houses in which Buddhas were installed. For instance, it is recorded in the *Nihon Shoki* that a certain Wakaomi-no-Azumabito of Shinano went to the capital in the days of the Emperor Kōgyoku and brought back an image of Buddha which he installed in his house, and this is the beginning of the famous temple of Zenkōji. It is not so remarkable that, situated as it is in a remote district, this temple should have preserved definite traces of the plan of an ancient residence, as pointed out by Dr. Kida in his research into the relations between temples, shrines, and residences in Japan. The Main Hall (Hondo) of the Zenkōji is a building 58 yards long from north to south, but only 30 yards wide from east to west. It has, of course, been considerably lengthened since it was first founded, and does not now resemble the original building; but Dr. Kida considers that the north end in which the image of Amida Buddha stands probably represents the early temple which was entered from the eastern end and was therefore a building just like that of the Izumo shrine. Afterwards, when the front entrance developed, this temple was altered to conform to the fashion. This inner part of the sanctuary measures just 18 feet square.

The type of house entered in front like the Ise shrine is the commonest and is found everywhere. The example here given is, however, a very old type at Hase in the neighborhood of Kyoto. The interior plan is still the same, but there is an addition at the side of an earthfloored kitchen space in which is the stove and a wooden bench *(shōgi)* at which meals are taken. This house has no verandas *(engawa)* except before the reception room. The walls are all of plaster, with few windows, and there is no ceiling. The Nando has plastered walls with no window and is quite dark. It was formerly actually used to sleep in, but is now only used as a storeroom. It is the custom in Kyoto, even in the large merchants' houses, for the master and his servants to take their meals on this wooden bench in the earth-floored kitchen court, a survival from the days before the floors were boarded and matted. The Shishinden (ceremonial hall) of the palace was formerly without a ceiling, which was in those days lacking everywhere. Most farm-houses and many dwellings in the towns also have still no ceiling in the kitchen and often in other rooms as well. And Japanese have always liked the effect of this open roof, properly dressed *(keshoyaneura),* and affect it much in verandas, tearooms and corridors.

These examples show that the shrine was simply the ancient Japanese residence and it will be noted, too, that farm-houses, like shrines, are very often surrounded by a grove. The word *mori* (grove) is explained by Miyasaki in his *Dictionary of Foreign Words* as equivalent to the Korean *ma-lin* meaning "forbidding" or "protecting." And in the *Manyoshu* the expression *kinden* (forbidden fields) is read in Japanese as *morita,* while the same text has *mori* for *jinja* (shrine). So *mori* is likely to mean the protecting hedge round a dwelling or shrine, and it is significant that the Deity Susa-no-O, who is an Izumo Deity, goes to Korea and lives in a place called Soshi-mori, the *mori* of which probably means "abode." And in the village of Tsutsu in Tsushima there is still to be seen a grove of oak-trees with an altar in the middle, which is exactly the same as the Shiki-no-Himorogi mentioned in the annals of the Emperor Sujin as erected to worship the Sun Goddess. This Himorogi is an enclosure of trees with an altar in the center in which the presence of the Deity is held to be manifest. It is still used where there is no shrine and it seems likely that it was the earliest place of worship before a residence was set aside for the Deity. The word *himorogi* is explained as equivalent to *mi-muro-gi* (trees of the divine abode) and *shiki* as the same as *suki,* also "abode." The grove in Tsushima is called Shiga by the villagers, which is quite likely the same word. This Himorogi is not peculiar to Japan either, for in the *Chou Li* in the days of Confucius a description of the same thing is found. It is just that worship "under the blue vault of heaven"[47] that many still prefer. And the Japanese Shinto shrine has never been a congregational building. It is the abode of the Deity which the worshippers approach but do not enter. Its later developments were entirely the result of the influence of the Buddhist connexion. Its resemblance to a Greek temple will no doubt already have occurred to most—except that it never housed an image but only a symbol. One may perhaps conjecture that the Izumo type of shrine, the square umbrella style, was introduced through Korean influence, while the Ise type represents a Polynesian variety that came in with the invaders from the south.

In the latter connexion mention may be made of the unique buildings at Iwase at Shirakawa, in the province of Hida on the borders of Shinano and Echizen, one of the most remote parts of the country deep in the mountain ranges where few outsiders have penetrated. These big residences contain a very large family including relations, more than thirty people in all, and look like a survival of the Polynesian long-house (in Japanese *nagaya* [long-house] is the word for barrack or tenement), in which a whole village community lives. And the roofs are extremely steep, some 60 degrees or more, just like that of the Izumo shrine and the older buildings before the less acute Chinese type of roof was introduced and popularized in the Nara period. Few of the more modern Japanese roofs have a slope of more than 45 degrees owing to this influence, and as the result of wood and tile coverings instead of the earlier thatch which shrines nearly always retain, though now it is usually thick shingle. The Emperor Yūryaku (A.D. 457-480), in whose days intercourse with the neighboring lands was very flourishing, is described as ordering a "storied pavilion" to be built, though no details are given of it. But in the days of the Emperor Suinin something of the kind was apparently not unknown because there is in the *Kōjiki* a passage in which his younger sister O-Naka-hime declares she cannot climb into the Ama-no-hokora because she is a weak woman and he replies that a ladder can be made. It must have been the sort of building depicted on the mirror dug up at Kariai village in the Katsuragi district of Yamato province. (Plate 1 Fig 2.) Polynesian houses, high like these early shrines, are often entered by a notched log which does not look very easy to climb. Yūryaku Tenno was contemporary with the Six Dynasties of China and in one of the works of this period, called *Liang Chou Lai Lien,* it is stated that they had communication with Pacific lands from a distance of five thousand *li* to twenty or thirty thousand.

Hokora is the Japanese word still used for a small shrine. It seems to contain the word *kura,* found in Taka-mi-kura (the Imperial Throne), which is like a small raised enclosure with a canopy. It may therefore mean "a raised place" and is compared by Fujita with the word *uran,* which is said to be used of a pavilion by some unknown southern country in the *Liang Dynasty Records of the Southern Countries.*

CHAPTER 3

The Introduction Of Buddhism
Asuka Period (540-640 A.D.)

It was the introduction of Buddhism that brought architecture to Japan with the crafts of painting and sculpture, metal-work and ceramics. Chinese writing may well have been known already, but not very much and to few people. Buddhism was first brought to Japan in 522 by one Shiba Tachito, a Chinese from Southern Liang, where it was very fashionable. He set up a chapel with an image and the great Minister Soga-no-Iname also gave his house to be used for the same purpose. Then in the sixth year of the Emperor Bidatsu (578) there arrived monks and Buddha-makers and temple artisans from Kudara, the western part of Korea. So the Minister Soga-no-Umako, son of Iname, was able to build a pagoda of some sort on the hill of Ono in Yamato, the first of many of its kind—but nothing remains of it but a few stones and tiles, for it was burnt by the opposition.

However, when Buddhists once more gained a footing, having overcome the objections of the conservative military party which was as anti-foreign and pro-Shinto as it usually is, a number of leading scholars came from the continent in the days of the Empress Suiko (593-628) equipped with all the knowledge of science and the arts as then developed; and before a century had passed since its first appearance Buddhism could count forty-six temples, eight hundred and sixty monks, and five hundred and sixty-nine nuns. But of this period little has been left but names, for the buildings themselves are of later date and only the Kondo (main hall), the pagoda, the middle gate, and the cloisters of the great monastery of Hōryuji, and the pagoda of the Hokkiji have survived. Indeed it is a wonder that so much is still to be seen, since they are all wooden buildings and in Japan fires and wars and earthquakes are endemic.

What is rather remarkable is that the Hōryuji is the only building that remains anywhere to show what the style of the wooden structures of the North and South dynasties in China, transmitted through Korea, was like. Similarly the Yume-dono of the same monastery is the only surviving ancient Korean building, for none are left in that country itself. Japan is indeed a museum of ancient Far Eastern civilizations.

The Hōryuji represents what is called the Kudara style "Temple of Seven Halls" (Kudara-shiki Shichido Garan), it was a combination of college and infirmary and temple. In front it had a large court or cloister and it faced the south. All these early temples are approached by a Nandaimon (Southern Great Gate). The great hall and the pagoda stand in the cloister and behind them is the library and the bell-tower. Behind this is the lecture hall (Kōdō) and on the north, east, and west are the residences of the monks.

There are two plans of this style, the one that has the main hall and pagoda built on a straight line running through the middle gate and lecture hall like the ancient Korean temples and the Shitennoji at Osaka in Japan, and the Hōryuji type that has them set on each side of this line. It is possible that these buildings may have been rebuilt after a fire as some allege; but even so there is no reason to doubt that they are anything but genuine specimens of Asuka work, for they are quite different from the productions of the Nara age.[48] Moreover, their decorations and the Buddhist statuary do not seem to have been damaged. A set of eaves has been added at a later date to the lower part of the Kondo for protection against the weather and the fenestration somewhat altered. Professor Amanuma's drawing represents it as it was in its original state. The dragon-carved struts in the upper part and the ornaments in the gable ends were added in the Edo period and look like it.[49] The Kondo stands on a stone base and its round pillars have entasis. They have no bases but stand on natural stones resembling the Greek Doric order. Their greatest diameter is about a third from the bottom, and they diminish in circumference only slightly toward the base, whereas they do so much more toward the top, their proportions being therefore not unlike those of the Corinthian column. On the top of the pillars are round plates *(sarato),* and on these again the bracket capitals. The pillars have no connexion with the upper story, the eaves have no ceiling, and the rafters no particular method of arrangement. The elbow brackets are of the simplest form, but at the corners they are prolonged in a cloud shape and are so called "cloud brackets" *(kumo hijiki)*. The simpler form is called "ship bracket" *(funo hijiki)*. Beneath the bressummer beam of the upper story is a species of strut that is the earliest form of the characteristic "frog-crotch" *(kaeru-mata)*. These details are almost exactly identical with those of the rock carvings of the Tat'ung caves in Shansi province in China, famous as survivals of the North Wei style of architecture which derived from the Gupta era in India (fifth century).[50]

The balustrade of the upper part has a swastika design which is also unique. It seems likely that the ridge had originally "kite-tail" terminals *(shibi)* like those of the Tamamushi shrine which is preserved in the Kondo. It is a model of a building of this type, 7 feet high, said to have been the private shrine of the Empress Suiko, and to have been formerly in the Tachibana temple. It has square pillars and round rafters, but in this only it differs from the Kondo. Its name comes from the covering of the wings of beetles *(tamamushi)* that once under the metal openwork overlay. The paintings on it are of Buddhist scenes done in Chinese style with some kind of oil. Altogether it is a very remarkable work of art.

The Hōryuji pagoda is the earliest in Japan. The Japanese word *to* (pagoda) is short for *sotoha,* from the Sanskrit *stupa*—just as the word *garan,* used in early days for Buddhist temples, is short for *sōgarama (sangharama)*. The purpose of this tower is either to indicate a sacred site or to contain a Buddhist relic. In Japan it was for the latter purpose and not simply for ornament. The Indian stupa is the mound-shaped tomb of a great person surmounted by a royal throne with an umbrella on top of it, as seen in Sanchi and the Ajanta cave chapels. In China and Japan the relic was originally in the receptacle on the pinnacle of the spire, so this part was considered the most important and emphasized accordingly, while the central member developed into the three, five, or seven stories that distinguish the Far Eastern variety. In China they are made of brick and stone; and smaller ones are sometimes found in

Japan of the latter material, but never full-sized ones. The stupa base has disappeared altogether in this ordinary type but appears again in the Daito and Hōto type introduced in the ninth century. This is of the same variety as the Tibetan *chorten,* with the difference that wooden construction naturally produces. In Japan the lowest story of a pagoda is used as a chapel and decorated in gilt and colors. This one is a five-storied structure with just the same architectural features as the Kondo and, like it, erected on a stone stylobate.

The colonnade that surrounds the cloister is very simply and harmoniously constructed with dressed rafters, exhibiting a very early form of *kōryo* or curved tie-beam connecting the tops of the pillars, on the heads of which are the three-branch brackets characteristic of this style. The lines of these brackets have the same gentle curve as the elbow, unlike those of later date. In the centre of this tie-beam is the same frog-crotch as is found in the balustrade. The pagoda of the Hokkiji is also a fine specimen and the largest of the three-storied variety. Its wide eaves have a comparatively gentle curve and its proportions are most graceful, more so in fact than any of similar type. Its details are the same as those of the Hōryuji.[51]

As to the Shi-Tennoji at Osaka, it has none of its original buildings left, though it was the first temple to be built, and was begun as the result of a vow by Prince Shōtoku that he would build a temple to the Four Deva Kings (Shi-Tenno) if he won the fight against Moriya, chief of the Mononobe or military caste. The present buildings are of the Momoyama and Edo periods, not earlier than the sixteenth century. But in their plan they have preserved the original form, and the Nandaimon (Great South Gate), the middle gate (Chūmon) the pagoda, the Kondo, and the Kōdō are all in a straight line in that order across the quadrangle. Shōtoku Taishi built seven temples beside the Shi-Tennoji and the Hōryuji. The Chuguji, the Tachibana-dera, the Hachioka-dera, the Ikejiri-dera, the Katsuragi-dera, for instance, and besides these there are the Kumagori, Yamaha, and Kume temples of this period, most of them, long ago destroyed or rebuilt. On the tiles of the Hōryuji and in some other parts of it are designs of honeysuckle and vine scrolls *(karakusa)* of the same kind as those in the

Parthenon and on Greek vases. The vine scroll pattern is not found in Korea and so has evidently come from Gandhara work by way of China. These temples were painted red with the ends of the beams yellow and the balustrades of the balconies green. The interiors were plastered and decorated in colors also—green, red, purple, black, and brown. There is little carved work in the Hōryuji. The ends of the rafters where they project are plain and have no elephant-headed ornaments or patterns like the later structures, but there are in some places metal mounts of openwork on these beams. The ends of the balustrade rails, again, are quite straight and have not the upward curve usually seen later.

The only architectural survivals of the Asuka era are therefore the temples, and nothing remains to show what the capital was like but tradition and a few foundation stones. According to this evidence the capital of Asuka lay across the plain south of Nara between Mount Unebi (near which is the mausoleum of Jimmu Tenno) and Ama-no-Kaguyama famous in the *Manyōshu*. It is conjectured that the city was laid out on the same plan as that of Nara, but with twelve avenues, the great central Shujaku Avenue leading to the Fujiwara palace of the Empress Jito and the Emperor Mommu, with the Daikyoku Den or Great Hall of Audience. Round about it are the mausolea of many Emperors. Judging from the architecture of the temples, the palace buildings might well have been quite imposing, though some also may have been of the simple style of the shrines, for there is mention of a Kuroki-no-miya (natural wood palace) by Tenchi Tenno (668), though this may have been a detached one. But the Asuka palace of the Empress Kōgyoku (642) was roofed with boards, and that of the Empress Saimei (655) was the first to be covered with tiles.

CHAPTER 4

Hakuhō Period (640-720 A.D.)

By this time the South and North period in China had given place to the Sui dynasty, a short one chiefly noted for the luxurious Emperor who built many temples and excavated the Grand Canal. Then this passed to make way for the famous dynasty of T'ang under the Emperor Tai Tsung, when the Middle Kingdom reached the zenith of her greatness and made her influence felt from the Yellow Sea to the confines of Persia.

Japan, as might be expected of her, at once threw herself whole-heartedly into importing and adapting this brilliant civilization to her own needs, and the Hakuhō[52] period was the result. The name Taika or Great Reform was given to this process of sinicization which was much the same as the Meiji Restoration of 1868, except that the T'ang culture was no doubt more compatible with conditions in Japan than was European, and its architecture more easily adapted than, for example, that of the continental Renaissance. It suited the climate and could be carried out in wood. Little remains now of the T'ang era in China except what is excavated or written, so that again we can see more of its works in Japan than in the country of its origin. There are no traces of Sui style in Japan, but at once in the Hakuhō period we find the T'ang variety of the Shichido Garan or Temple of Seven Halls.

This has two pagodas facing each other, often inside the quadrangle, at a little distance from the center line of the buildings through the south gate, which is as before. In the earlier day they are not as regular as in the later Tempyo period: for example, the Kōfukuji at Nara has its eastern pagoda of four stories and its western of three. At Yakushiji both are similarly placed inside the cloister as in the Kudara style, so that it may be said that this period has the character of a transition from Asuka to Tempyo. The buildings stand on a stone stylobate with square bases to the pillars which have a slight entasis. Square pillars are used in the upper story and the bracketing is three-branched.

The buildings of the Kōfukuji, built by Fujiwara Fuhito in 712 as a chapel for his family, are all modern, for it has been burnt many times. But a remarkable relic of this time is the three-storied pagoda at Yakushiji. Originally there were two, but only the eastern pagoda has survived, and of the western only the foundation stones remain. The detail of the bracketing is reminiscent of the Asuka style, but the eaves are ceiled and the lowest chamber has a coved ceiling, both innovations. It is unique among Japanese pagodas for having double eaves to each story, the same construction as the roof of the Hōryuji Kondo, and a throw-back to the Asuka style. Japanese critics consider it very elegant and rhythmic in its proportions and one writer lauds it as "frozen music." This peculiarity gives it the appearance of having six stories, an even number, whereas all others except the Tahōtō type have an odd number of stories. It is 120 feet high, the *sōrin* or spire comprising 20 feet of this and having on its top an elaborate iron "spray" like the decoration of a weathercock; but with a design of three Buddhist angels with flowing robes, one playing a flute, the second scattering perfume, and the third lotus flowers. A very interesting relic is the model pagoda of the Kairyuōji, now in the Nara museum, a miniature edition of the actual edifice which has fortunately escaped destruction. It must be one of the oldest wooden architectural models in existence. The dearth of relics of this age is mostly due to the removal of the capital to Nara, whither some of the buildings were transferred, but most were allowed to fall into ruin.

CHAPTER 5

Tempyo Period (720-780 A.D.)

THE Emperor Mommu had decided to move the capital again and in the reign of his successor, the Empress Gemmyo, it was changed to the site of Nara on the north side of the plain under the foot of Mount Mikasa, and here it remained until 794, during the reigns of seven Sovereigns. This is the golden age of Buddhist architecture and sculpture for more of the resources of the country were spent on these things than ever afterwards. This was because of the immense enthusiasm of the Sovereign and the Court for the Indian philosophy. Nara was certainly a city of monks and temples, and a contemporary account says that, looking down on it from Wakagusa hill more than fifty pagodas could be counted rearing their graceful spires aloft, conspicuous among them the two great seven-storied ones of the Tōdaiji, 320 feet high, and another at the Gankōji of 240 feet. Nara had seven great temples: the Tōdaiji, the Saidaiji, the Daianji, the Kōfukuji, the Gankōji, the Yakushiji, and the Toshōdaiji. But of all their extensive buildings but little now remains. Even the Great Buddha of the Tōdaiji has been burnt three times and his head melted off, so that only his body is of this period.

By this time the T'ang type of temple had been perfected and the twin eastern and western pagodas stood outside the cloister equidistant on east and west. The Kondo stood in the center of the quadrangle of the first court entered by the middle gate through the outer south gate as before. Through a second gate lay the inner court in which were the belfry and the library, equidistant from the axis of the court. Behind these again was the Kōdō. The details of the construction are now fully developed, but entirely functional and quite without fussiness. The pillars are round with a slight bulge and the bracket capitals of the three-branch type. The soffits of the rafters and the interior ceilings are coved and ribbed *(shirin)*. The curved ties have simple uncarved frog-crotches and straight struts alternating with them. The spacing of the pillars and the fenestration give these buildings a very restful and dignified air, as can be well seen from the façades of the Kondo and Kōdō of the Toshōdaiji. The latter building is said to have been one of the halls of the Imperial Palace which was presented to this temple. The Great Buddha Hall or Kondo of the Tōdaiji is the largest wooden building in the world, but it does not belong to this period, since it was reconstructed in the Tenjiku style of the Kamakura era. Only part of the Hokkedo (a wing was added to it in the Kamakura style), the library of the Kangakuin, and the Tengai gate of this temple are of the Nara age. The finest specimens of the period are the Toshōdaiji, the Yume-dono and library and refectory of the Hōryuji, the eastern pagoda of the Tomado and the octagonal hall (Hakkakudo) of the Eisanji. The Hokkedo is really older than the Tōdaiji itself, for it was built by Archbishop Ryōben in the fifth year of Tempyo (733) and has survived all the rest.

The Toshōdaiji was the work of Kanshin, a Chinese monk, on the site of the residence of Prince Nitabe which the Emperor Shōmu gave him. Its Kondo is perhaps the finest specimen of the architecture of the Nara age. As in all the other temples, the roof is of the single *azumaya* or hipped type with kite-tail finials. In the front the pillars are arranged to form a colonnade. It was painted red outside with green window bars and the cove of the ceiling was decorated with vine scroll patterns and Buddhist figures, while the pillars are also ornamented with designs of flowers and flying Bodhisats.

The Kōdo was originally, it is said, the Chōshuden of the palace, presented by the Empress Kōken of great piety. Among other things it had originally no ceiling, only the tie-beam and frog-crotch construction under the dressed rafters; but when rebuilt as the lecture hall of the temple a coffered ceiling was added. The doors and lattice windows are of the Kamakura age and the bracketing and struts have also been altered somewhat. The 240-foot pagoda of the Gankōji and the main hall were standing until the eighteen-twenties when they were burnt, but a woodcut that remains, reproduced by Professor Amanuma, shows very fine and stately proportions.

Nara also contains one quite unique structure, the Shōsōin or log-built storehouse in which have reposed, ever since the death of the Emperor Shōmu, all the furniture and utensils that he had used and which were presented to the Tōdaiji by the Empress Kōmyo for the perfection of his enlightenment. There were many other store-houses of the same construction in other temples too, but few have survived and it is remarkably providential that this one, the most valuable of all, should have been preserved, though it has had some narrow escapes.[53] There is no other collection in the world like it, for these are not excavated objects, but have always been above ground where they now are and their condition is excellent. They have been cataloged and annotated and there are some three thousand articles in all,[54] comprising furniture, dress, weapons, food utensils, games, musical instruments and writings, pictures and Buddhist statuettes. Besides objects of Japanese workmanship they include Korean, Chinese, and even Indian and Persian specimens presented to the Chinese Emperor, and thence sent to Japan. Belonging to the Imperial Household, they could not be viewed even by the Shogun without the Imperial Permission. This construction of logs is called Azekura[55] and is made of three-cornered lengths interlocked. It stands on big round pillars 9 feet high on large stone bases. The space beneath it gives good ventilation and the method of construction is such that in summer the heat contracts the timbers and lets in the breeze through the interstices, while in winter the damp expands them and keeps the interior dry. And as the projecting edges of these beams are triangular the birds are quite unable to build nests in them. All these qualities, say the Japanese commentators, make this Azekura style ideal for storehouses. The timber is *hinoki* and it is worn down an inch and a half outside by the weathering of some twelve hundred and fifty years.

Within the precincts of the Hōryuji are preserved two other fine relics of the Tempyo age. These are the Yume-dono and the Dempōdō of the Tōin temple built in 739 on the site of the Ikaruga palace of Prince Shōtoku. The Yume-dono (Hall of Dreams) is the Kondo of the temple and the Dempōdō is the Kōdō. The former is a graceful octagonal building standing on a stone stylobate of two tiers with a railed veranda round it. The interior has a stone floor and a base made of a kind of concrete. On the top of the roof, which is of the pyramidal type, there is an uncommon finial consisting of a jar-shaped vessel on a lotus throne having a canopy with wind-bells over it, and on that again a jewel top. It is the *kalasha* or nectar pot (called also by the Japanese *rōban* or dew pot, the first syllable being for *kanrō* or nectar) which is a feature of the spires of Hindu temples.[56] There is another on the top of the pagoda of the Murōji, but this is the earliest and they are rare. The Dempōdō is interesting also for having been, according to tradition, the residence of the Lady Tachibana, mother of the Empress Kōmyo. It is a single-roofed gabled building with a veranda in front and a wooden floor, neither of which things are found in the temple halls of this age. Thus it is a rare specimen of the residence of a noble in the early eighth century. Of a similar type is the Kondo of the Shin-Yakushiji, burnt after a few years, but rebuilt soon afterwards. The pagoda and the rest of it are of the Kamakura age. It is peculiar in having a round Buddha altar stuccoed in white standing on the usual stone floor.

On the whole, the interior decoration of this period is far more developed than that of the previous ones. The pillars and ceilings are very finely painted and the outside is red as before. There is little if any carving in the temples and only some openwork metal mounts. All this color is, of course, quite continental, and Japanese taste had not yet eliminated it.

The Capital Of Heijo

Owing to the greater solidity of the architecture as well as the increasing complication of life that had resulted from the introduction of continental civilization and the improvement of communications, it seems to have been felt that the shifting of the capital with the reign was far from convenient. So when, in 708, the capital was moved to Nara, a far more permanent kind of building was adopted both for the palace and for the better class of residence. By 724 the palace and the great temples had been rebuilt there. Other structures must have been of a more temporary nature, for an edict was issued by the Dajokan or Cabinet suggesting that officials of the fifth rank and upwards and other substantial families should roof their houses with tiles, plaster them white, and paint them red.

This capital has of course quite disappeared but, principally through the investigations of Professors Kida and Sekino, most of its details have been made fairly clear except in some cases—as for instance the width of the streets. It was laid out on the model of the T'ang capital of Chang An, but its greatest length was from north to south instead of from east to west as in that city, while the use of numbers for its streets instead of names was a Japanese innovation. It was laid out in the Handen or checker-board fashion, i.e. divided into *jō* or avenues of four *chō* in width, east to west and north to south. These *jō* were again divided into *bō* of four *chō* square, sixteen *chō* thus going to a *bō*. These were again divided into sixteen *tsubo*. The city was nine *jō* from north to south and eight *bō* from east to west. Right down the middle from the south gate to the gate of the government quarter in the north ran the wide central highway called the Shujaku, dividing the city into the left and right capitals (Sakyo and Ukyo). Then every four *chō*, parallel with the Shujaku went another wide street *(ōji)* while narrow streets *(koji)* divided the *chō*. The wide street at the end of the fourth *bō* was called *Kyōgoku* or City Limit. From the second avenue of the left capital to the fifth was an extension of three *bō* called the outer capital (Gekyo) within which the great temples of the Kōfukuji, and Gankōji were situated. The Imperial Enclosure occupied four *chō* at the north end. On the south side of it was the Shujaku gate, and twelve other gates gave entrance to it on the four sides. Within was the palace with the Chōdōin and Daikyoku Den or Halls of Ceremony and Audience, where the great festivals were held and entertainments were given. The foundations of many of these buildings have been excavated recently and their sites determined, but with the exceptions above mentioned nothing is left of them. Probably they were not very different from those of Heian. The palace itself was built on an elevation with a view of the Yamato mountains.

CHAPTER 6

Heian Period (780-1190 A.D.)

The Heian period comprises the four centuries that elapsed from the removal of the capital from Nara to the fall of the Heike house, perhaps more accurately 805-1192. The influence of the T'ang civilization still continued, but a very considerable modification was caused by the introduction of Tendai and Shingon Buddhism—the Esoteric System (Mikkyo), as it is called—by the two great ecclesiastics Dengyo and Kōbō. Moreover the T'angs were decidedly on the decline and so Japan ceased to regard them with the same respect as formerly. The Shingon strain brought in a more austere type of building, and soon after this the intercourse with the T'angs ceased altogether and the golden age of the Fujiwara Regents inaugurated a more luxurious habit of building and developed incidentally a pure Japanese style by eliminating all that was not in accordance with the national taste.

This period is conveniently divided into the first century from the foundation of the Heian capital to the accession of the Emperor Uda in 897, called the Kōnin era, and the later three centuries from that time to 1192, usually known as the Fujiwara period—four centuries of peace and prosperity, and for the Court and officials considerable luxury, in which the arts and crafts could be cultivated. The first period is a transition from Tempyo to Fujiwara, rather like the early Nara age that led up to Tempyo.

Tendai Buddhism was founded by Dengyo Daishi who went to China and studied on Mount Tientai, whence the name, and Shingon or Tantric Buddhism by Kōbō Daishi who also went there[57] and these sects required a different kind of temple from those so far prevailing. Denyo built Hieizan on the mountain of that name to the northwest of the capital, to protect it from the demons who are reputed to attack from that quarter, though later on the monks assumed their function: but Kōbō founded his establishment on Mount Koya in the province of Kii, far from all inhabited parts. A flat site in a capital was not a suitable place to meditate on profound philosophies; and since these remote mountain peaks were chosen for monasteries it was not possible to keep to the older conventional regular form at all. The monasteries had to be arranged to fit their environment, and the halls placed often on different levels, where any small flat place for them could be found: "sites in the hills no bigger than a cat's forehead," is the Japanese description. There were very few places like Mount Koya, where there is quite an extensive plateau on the hill. Most were like Hieizan, where the buildings were scattered irregularly up and down, and in some cases had to be built out from the rocks and supported on trestles from below.

This age saw the introduction of a new kind of pagoda. This was the Daito which had a square lower story with the usual pyramidal roof; but superimposed on this, as though emerging from it, is a round dome called a "turtle belly," crowned by a round balustrade over which again is a roof with a spire supported on pillars. There are also two other varieties of stupa, the Sōrinto and the Yūgito, the former a Tendai speciality and the latter peculiar to Shingon. The Sōrinto is a simple stupa pillar or *stambha*[58] and the Yūgito, named after Yūgi Bosatsu because a picture of it is on a portrait of him, is a stupa reliquary with a top like that of the Daito, but with a round base with doors under the turtle's belly, the whole standing on a turtle's back. On the roof are five spires, one on each angle of it and one in the middle. It is described as a pagoda of five peaks and eight pillars, symbolical perhaps of the Noble Eightfold Path and the Five Prohibitions. Professor Amanuma, who, from an old picture, has constructed one lately at the Ryūkoin, the temple on Mount Koya where Kōbō Daishi lived, points out that the Amravati Dagoba has four pillars a side with a rail between in just this style.

The great temples of this early Kōnin era were the Enryakuji on Mount Hiei, the Kongobuji on Mount Kōya, and the Kyōō Gōkokuji now called Tōji, Ninnaji, Murōji, and Kiyomizu-dera in Kyoto; but all that remains of the period is the Kondo and five-storied pagoda of the Murōji. There was a decided development of shrine architecture at this time under the influence of Buddhism. The types that are new are the Kasuga style, the Nagare or Yuiitsu style, the Hiyoshi and the Hachiman styles.

The Kasuga shrine is a gabled building with a lean-to porch supported on pillars and covering the front steps, which are in the center of the gable. The roof, like that of most shrines, now takes on the curve associated with Buddhist temples. The Shimmei style is merely a modified form of the Ise type, with one side of the roof brought right forward over the front steps, and more ornamental balustrades. Both this and the former one are painted red, thus departing from the simplicity of the plain grey wood of Ise and Izumo. The Kamo shrine, too, is of this type. The actual buildings of these shrines are not old, but like Ise and Izumo shrines they have always been rebuilt in the same form. In these later types the characteristic cross-beams (*chigi* and *katsuōgi*) are omitted and the roof approximates to that of a temple; or if they are present they are not functional at all but merely applied ornaments. The Hachiman style has a gabled shrine 18 feet deep, with a second one 6 feet deep built in front of it and connected with it by an ante-chamber. The Hiyoshi type is an 18-foot-deep shrine with the roof brought down over the steps in front and eaves projecting on both sides, looking like an *irimoya* roof at the ends and a gabled one in front. It has a veranda round it.

The Heian Capital

The Emperor Kammu moved the capital from Nara to Nagaoka in Yamashiro in 784; and there it remained for ten years, when it was moved once more to the village of Uda, also in Yamashiro province, where the new palace and city were built and finished by 804. This was called the Capital of Heian (Heian no Miyako), usually called Miyako or "the Capital" since it continued to be so till 1870 when the military capital of Edo became the Imperial Residence under the name of Tokyo or Eastern Capital. The old capital was then called Kyoto, or very often Saikyo or Western Capital by the people of western Japan, just as Nara was usually known in medieval times as Nankyo or Southern Capital.

The reason for the change is said to have been the Emperor's desire to escape from the oppressive atmosphere of the monasteries of Nara.

The new site was certainly a good one, a flat plain by the river Kamo which communicated with the river Yodo and the sea, surrounded by hills on the east, west, and north and comparatively close to Lake Biwa to the east. The other sites had not been so well supplied with waterways. The new city was laid out on the same plan as that of Nara, with the Shujaku highway down the center dividing it into left and right capitals. It was about three and a half miles long north to south and three miles east to west. It had the same nine avenues. The Great Highway was 250 feet wide and the other avenues were 80 feet wide, except the first and ninth (Ichijo and Kujo) which were 120, Nijo, which was 170, and four others between the first and ninth, which were 100 feet wide. Similarly the transverse streets running parallel with the Shujaku, those at the extremities, the east and west Kyōgoku, and two others were 120 and the rest 80 feet wide. The smaller lanes were 40 feet wide. The city unit was a block of 400 feet square called a *chō,* which was normally divided into thirty-two residential areas of 50 by 100 feet. Four of these blocks went to a *hō* or square and again four *hō* made a *bō* or division. The *bō* was the square space between two *jō* or avenues, and there were four of them, as in Nara, between the Great Highway and the Kyōgoku or city boundary on the east and west. On the south at the end of the central highway was the Rashomon or Great Gate of the city, 54 feet wide with seven portals: while at the north end, as before, was the Shujaku gate of the palace enclosure.

The whole city was surrounded by an embankment and ditch and was intersected from south to north by the east and west Horikawa, the east and west Omiyagawa, the Sakigawa, and the west Dōingawa streams, which were canalized and made to flow so that they added considerably to the amenities of the city. On each side of the Rashomon stood the East and West Temples, Tōji and Saiji, and in front of the palace enclosure was the Imperial Pleasure Park (Shinen) and the University (Daigaku). The palace enclosure extended from Ichijo to Nijo, 1,533 yards from north to south and 1,266 from east to west within were the Dairi or Imperial Residence and all the government departments as before. There were fourteen gates, four on the east and west and three on the south and north sides.

Two large buildings inside the palace were the Chōdōin, used for the accession ceremony and other important Court functions, and the Burakuin where the Imperial Entertainments were held. The first had a front court with two towers projecting into it beside the main gate and within were the East and West Chōshuden Halls. A second gate led into a larger court with twelve more halls, four on each side and four in the middle. Lastly behind that was a third court with the Daikyoku Den or Grand Throne Hall, with a smaller one, the Shōanden, behind it. On the right and left of the Daikyoku Den were the towers of the Geen Dragon and White Tiger. It was a building 22 yards square with a hipped roof covered with green tiles with kite-tail finials at each end of the ridge. The floor was also tiled and in the center stood the Imperial Throne. The Daikyoku Den was burnt many times and was not rebuilt after the last fire in 1177. Recently a replica of it has been put up in Kyoto. The Chōdōin was set right in front of the Shujaku gate on the southwest of the palace. The Burakuin was 22 yards square and had a dais for the throne in the center. In front and on each side were three smaller halls and behind it three more in a row on each side connected by colonnaded corridors. It was sum rounded by a wall making an enclosure 112 yards east to west and 296 yards south to north. It was burnt and not rebuilt after 1063.

The ceremonies that had been performed in the Daikyoku Den were afterwards transferred to the Shishinden, the Front Hall of Audience in the palace itself. The palace had twelve gates as before and the Shishinden lay facing the Kenrei-mon or front gate across the courtyard. It is 90 feet east to west and 75 feet north to south. It has an inside corridor under the eaves and an inner chamber in the middle in which is the throne. The roof is of dressed rafters without a ceiling and on the north side are sliding screens painted with the figures of the great Chinese sages. It was burnt in 1227 and not rebuilt for a long time; the present structure dates from 1790. Restored exactly on the ancient model when the whole palace was rebuilt by the great Minister Matsudaira Sadanobu, the greatest pains were taken to get exact plans and information so that the style of the tenth century could be reproduced. After calling for tenders for the work Sadanobu accepted the highest one on the grounds that for fine construction a high price must be paid, and to consider anything else would show want of respect for the Court.

The actual residence of the Emperor was formerly the Jijuden, behind the Shishinden; but afterwards it was transferred to the Seiryoden which is a building of no great size—about 60 feet long by 30 feet wide. Inside is a main chamber which was the Imperial Livingroom, one corner of it floored with earth on which it was necessary for His Majesty to stand when worshipping the Sun Goddess and other Deities. Next to this was the dining room, the bedchamber and an anteroom and behind this were the apartments for the Consorts. Adjacent were bathroom, dressing-room and lavatory, and at the back the kitchen and the entrance. The simple life of the Emperors of that time is very evident from these by no means elaborate arrangements.

It was in this age that the new dogma (probably invented in the preceding period by Gyōgi, but strongly advanced now by Kōbō and Dengyo) that Shinto gods were manifestations of Buddha in Japan began to produce what is called Ryōbu Shinto or Double-faced Shinto, that is to say a Shinto in which the gods become, as it were, adopted children of Buddha. This affected the architecture of the shrines which began to assume storied gates, pagodas, quadrangles, elaborate carvings, and other appurtenances associated with Buddhism, while Buddhist monks often took charge of them—with the exception of the Ise shrine which never altered its ancient ways and where Buddhist monks were not even allowed to enter the precincts.

Though Hieizan was completely destroyed by Nobunaga in the late sixteenth century, Kōya San still survives as a specimen of these great groups of temples. It is very much like a Japanese equivalent of Oxford or Cambridge, though without any satellite residential town. Fish and women were rigidly excluded from Mount Koya up till 1870 and the latter are so still, though oddly enough liquor is not. But Hieizan was never so strict and it was not only monks that Nobunaga burnt. The great pagoda of Mount Koya was burnt in the nineteenth century, but some fifty temples remain, built with quadrangles with chapels and apartments for the many pilgrims who resorted there and special suites for the Imperial Envoys and feudal lords. In these apartments may be seen some of the finest speciments of Japanese interior decoration of the feudal age still actually in use. The mighty kitchens and bathrooms are interesting also, and the living-rooms contain a flue of plaster built over the hearth in the middle of the room to carry away the smoke or fumes—which I have neither seen nor heard of anywhere else in the country.

At the end of the long road that runs through the settlement is the mausoleum of Kōbō Daishi where, according to current belief, he sits in a long trance awaiting the coming of Maitreyya, the Buddhist Messiah. In front of it is a Hall of Lamps where lights burn perpetually; they have been dedicated by many famous people, and there is one that has never yet been extinguished since it was kindled by the Emperor Go-Shirakawa in the twelfth century, so it is said. Along the road has grown up a cemetery[59] where all the great of Japan have supernumerary tombs, thus assuring them the advantage of being in the van as usual when Kōbō rises. By the side of the Hall of Lamps is the Hall of Bones, a species of large letter-box in which the ashes of ordinary people may be deposited by their friends when they make the pilgrimage. The ashes are enclosed in a small earthen pot for the purpose. The roofs of the temple buildings here are covered with thick shingle like those of shrines, and certainly blend beautifully with the cryptomeria and other trees that surround them.

In the second part of this period, when the Fujiwara house held sway, architecture began to be assimilated to the national taste. By some three centuries are divided into an early part from 900 to 1100, and a later from 1100 to 1192. But actually it was a gradual progress without definite lines of demarcation. In the temples a new phenomenon was the Amida Hall. With the end of the intercourse with T'ang and the comparative waning of the attractions of the esoteric sects, partly owing to strife which broke out among them, the easy-going cult of Amida Buddha began to make much more headway. It has been suggested that it is derived somehow from Christianity, as it has also been maintained that Kōbō's doctrine is a form of gnosticism. But there is no cogent evidence for either view and the natural tendencies of human nature seem sufficient to explain Amidism. Shingon promised enlightenment through ritual and gesture; but the Amida scriptures promised it through something much easier—just faith in Amida Buddha and repetition of the formula of appeal to him. It promised something more attractive to the ordinary man than enlightenment, for it had a fine Paradise in the West (Saihō Jōdō, the Pure Western Land) to which believers would be fetched at death by Amida and his attendant Bodhisats riding on purple clouds of glory and playing on musical instruments. The paradise as despicted in art was evidently modelled on the Imperial Palace,[60] so the Fujiwara courtiers would naturally feel at home in it, and probably consider they had a prescriptive right to it from their support of temple fund while it gave the ordinary man what such conceptions always do, the prospect of living in luxury without work. Amida was said even to have a boat of his own to transport the elect over the river of the underworld, thus saving them the fee placed in the month of all others for the infernal ferryman. There was nothing esoteric about all this; every one was welcome and was cordially invited by propaganda. So the temples became rather of a congregational type with an Amida Hall, containing only his image, and a large matted space where people could sit and listen to exhortations and descriptions of paradise out of the Amida texts. It is easy to see why it became the most popular sect with all classes, as it still is, though later on Zen supplanted it with the military caste. But this era was one in which they had not yet become important.

Another development of this period was the Shinde style of residence. It was that used by the Fujiwara courtiers and had developed from the Imperial Palace, which was an elaborate form of it. Shinden was the name of the principal chamber in the center facing south, corresponding to the Shishinden of the place.[61] On each side of this and connected by covered corridors were subsidiary buildings called *tai* or "houses opposite." From these, two long covered ways at right angles enclosed the garden and extended to the lake in the middle of it, ending in an Izumi Dono and a Tsuri Dono—pavilions for cooling oneself and fishing respectively. In these covered ways were the "middle gates" for entry and exit. In the center of the lake was an island with bridges connecting it with either bank. Behind the main buildings, and again connected with them by bridges and covered ways, were the rooms for the ladies and the family. A very good example of a large specimen of this type is the Kanin Detached Palace which was what was called a Sato Dairi or country palace where the Emperor could live outside the city, and where many were forced to live when the main palace was burnt in the military turmoils. The custom started when the Emperor Murakami in 961 went to live in the Reizeiin mansion after a fire. After another fire or so the Sovereigns found it pleasant to live outside in the mansions of the Regents and stayed there for years, so they decided to build Detached Palaces of their own, and the number of these increased till in time there were more than twenty of them.

The Byōdōin temple at Uji is an example of a residence of this time that has survived, for it was originally the villa of the Regent Fujiwara Yorimichi, which he afterwards turned into a temple. There were the usual subsidiary buildings, but they got burnt and the Hō-ō-do or Phoenix Hall, as it is called from the resemblance of its outline to this Imperial Bird, is the only part that is left (though the Hō-ō is hardly a phoenix). It is an excellent example of the way in which the Fujiwara nobles planned to ensure good fortune in this world and the next. The nobles were most assiduous in building big temples—an example the Emperors and Retired Emperors and their Consorts all imitated, so Michinaga's Hoshōji and Yorimichi's Byōdōin were followed by the six *shōji* built by the Emperors Shirakawa, Toba, Sutoku, and Konoe and the Dowager Empress Taikenmonin, in which the influence of the palace style on that of the temple is very apparent.

The size of a noble's mansion was limited to one *bō*, i.e. 400 feet square. The Kanin palace is 840 north to south and 400 east to west. It was the largest of the country palaces. The size of the Shinden[62] or main chamber of a residence varied from 72 feet square to 42 and 30.[63] *Shitomi* or wooden gratings such as are still seen in Shinto shrines, with the upper half hinged at the top to open outwards, were used to close in the outside when necessary, though these were not allowed in the houses of ordinary folk. Inside were curtains and screens to divide the rooms, and there were mats here and there on the boarded floor for the great ones to sit on. Ordinary houses had wooden doors and only a main building without extensions or pavilions. All were very largely open to the air like roofed verandas, and the modern Japanese house is very little different. What has been added is the result of the Zen architecture of the next period plus the extension of the use of mats in town houses. But a Japanese of the present day could live in one of these houses of the tenth century without any discomfort. These were the residences in which the authoresses Murasaki and Sei Shonagon lived and in which Prince Genji and his friends spent their elegant existences. The Regent Michinaga was famous for the mansion he built at Kyōgoku and the others strove to emulate the grandeur of this most splendid of the Fujiwaras. But all this had no effect on the ways of the common people who continued for long to live in small and primitive thatched huts and cottages.

The interior decorations of this period as we see them where they have survived in the Hō-ō-do at Uji and in the Chusonji at Hiraizumi are very brilliant, all the wall space and pillars being painted and lacquered in gold and colors over wood and stucco, or inlaid with mother-of-pearl with ornaments of ivory and enamel. By this time the art of lacquering had advanced very far and fine work could be done in gold and various colors. Of the pillars, some are round with entasis and others square with bevelled corners, the bevel being about a fifth of the width of the pillar. The arched windows in the Hō-ō-do are of the Kamakura period and were evidently added afterwards.

Some of the frog-crotch struts in these buildings are of quite a different shape from those of the previous periods, though the older solid one is still found. The new type justifies its name much better for it is high and hollow and in some cases made of two pieces of wood joined in the middle. Those of the Chusonji, of this type, are covered with gold leaf over lacquer so that it is not possible to say whether they are one piece or two. Again, some of them have a little carving inside and it is from this kind that the extremely elaborate carved ones of the later periods developed. The roofs are hipped or hipped gable *(irimoya)* and the kite-tail finial is no longer found. For some time it seems to have been confined to the buildings in the Imperial Enclosure and now the "devil-headed" tile *(oni-gawara)* takes its place. This is an aeroterion with a grotesque face in relief on it; but when flat and without this decoration it is still called "devil-plate" finial, as the place where the devil ought to be.

The Chusonji at Hiraizumi is a remarkable survival from the great temple built by Fujiwara Kiyohira in 1094. He and his son and grandson, Motohira and Hidehira, built and maintained the provincial capital of this northern province on the same lines as the real one. They were a branch of this courtier family who had become Lords of the Marches against the barbarian Emishi and so had specialized in militarism. Its two temples, the Chusonji and the Moetsuji, were among the finest in the land, the former being an imitation of the *shōji* temples of Kyoto. There were others in the manner of the Byodoin and the Sanjusangendo at Kyoto, and there were shrines like those of Gion and Fushimi Inari. Groves of cherry-trees were planted to look like Higashiyama and in the middle of it all stood the mansion of Hidehira.

The Chusonji had some forty buildings altogether, but all that is left is this brilliantly decorated Kondo and the library. The Kondo is an Amida Hall and in the center of it the Buddha sits under the golden splendor of his canopy and the great pillars that support the 50-foot-high roof. All the beams and brackets are inlaid with mother-of-pearl and the metal mounts with cloisonné work. This building is an important one in another sense, in that it is the mausoleum shrine of the three generations of Fujiwara lords whose ashes are deposited under the altar; and from this idea in time developed the imposing mausolea of the Tokugawa Shoguns in the Edo period. But the actual plan of these, known as Gongen-zukuri, named after the "old Gongen" Ieyasu, originated in the Kaisando of Founder's Hall of the Eihōji temple of the Zen sect of the Muromachi period.

The five-storied pagoda of the Daigōji, finished in 936, is an interesting survival of this period, too, with the Hokkedo and Saihōdō of the same temple. It is 78 feet 4 inches high and the *sōrin* is 41 feet, rather more than a third of the height of the whole and more than half that of the body, making it the tallest spire on any pagoda. The interior of the lower story, ceiling, walls, and pillars is profusely decorated with pictures of Bodhisattvas and vine-leaf and lotus blossom designs, shading off from one color to the other *(bokashi)*.

No doubt the pagodas of the Yakushiji and the Toshōdaiji and other temples were similarly decorated, while the later example of the Hō-ō-do shows a further maturity. The Fukiji and Hakusui are specimens of the Amida-do of this period. The former has the boat-shaped elbow bracket of the Asuka age, which still sometimes persists, and a coffered ceiling above the Naijin or sanctuary. It has a pyramidal roof with a nectar-pot and jewel on the summit.

CHAPTER 7

Kamakura Period (1190-1340 A.D.)

IN the Kamakura era there was a renewal of the intercourse with China that had been interrupted in the later years of the T'ang period and several new sects of Buddhism were introduced. To the Six Sects of Nara and the two more esoteric sects of Heian were now added six more, Zen, Ji, Shin, Nichiren, Jōdō, and Yuzu Nembutsu, and with them came new styles of architecture derived from the Sung dynasty that was then flourishing in China. These were the Tenjiku (Indian) and the Kara (Chinese), and in contradistinction from them the type that had grown up in the Fujiwara period was called Wa or Japanese. Actually these new styles were, like all other Buddhist architecture, of Indian origin modified in China, and the names have no special connexion with any particular details. Before long the Tenjiku merged into the Wa style and lost its individuality, and then the Kara mode combined with the Wa to form a new style that prevailed from the end of the Kamakura right on into the Muromachi period. Tenjiku was the style chosen by the famous monk Jōgen in which to rebuild the Great Buddha Hall of the Tōdaiji after it had been burnt by Taira Shigehira in the Gempei wars; but, largely because it was thus started in Yamato where the Wa style was very popular, it was soon absorbed by this latter.

The Kara style especially associated with Zen, however, was introduced into Kyoto and Kamakura; and since the Zen sect was soon adopted by the dominant military caste as particularly suited to their spiritual needs, its characteristic architecture also held its own and had considerable influence on the buildings of succeeding ages.

It must be remembered that this was the period when the new military dictatorship of Japan was inaugurated under Minamoto Yoritomo, who, after vanquishing the other great military clan of the Taira (that had held sway for the previous thirty years) obtained from the Emperor an edict making over the administration of the whole country to him as Shogun or Commander-in-Chief. This office became hereditary in his family, the Minamoto, and remained so till 1868.

The first great Zen temples of the Kara style in Kyoto founded by the monks Eisai and Dōgen were the Nanzenji and the Daitokuji. Then came the Five Temples, first in Kyoto, and then a second edition in Kamakura, the military capital that Yoritomo set up in the east. These were the Tenryuji, Sōkokuji, Kenninji, Tōfukuji, and Manjuji in Kyoto and the Kenchoji, Engakuji, Jūfukuji, Jōchiji and Jōmyoji in Kamakura.

These Zen temples were quite different both in plan and detail from what had preceded them. Entering from the south there is the Sammon[64] or Great Two-storied Gate, then the Butsuden or Buddha Hall, the Hatto or Doctrine Hall, and the Hōjō or Residence, all in one straight line on the axis of the gate, while on the left and right inside the gate, in place of the two pagodas of the Nara age, were the Tōsu or latrines and the Yokushitsu or bath house. The library and bell-tower and Zendo or Meditation Hall were also located on each side as convenient. Often there was a lotus pool with a stone bridge over it outside the Sammon and a front gate (Sōmon) before that. As far as the regular plan went it was like a return to the Shitennōji style, but the details were quite different. The pillars sometimes had a stone base on the foundation stones and the floor was of square stone slabs laid diagonally. The pillars were tapered at the top and bottom (the form called *chimaki,* an elongated rice-cake narrower at the ends). They were the same shape in the Tenjiku style too, but here the taper was only at the top, though occasionally there are exceptions. The brackets are more sharply curved also. Then instead of frog-crotches or struts, clusters of brackets are used to support the beams between pillars, these clusters being in some cases almost continuous. This arrangement is called *tsume-gumi* or closed-bracketing. Ornamental brackets and capitals are also used in this style. Another characteristic is the spreading of the rafters like a fan in the upperstory of a two-story building and elsewhere. The projecting ends of the rafters at the corners are bevelled or tapered and not cut straight as before.

The ornamental window *(kato-mado,* flower-headed, or sometimes flame-headed, window) with an ogival top is first found in this period, and the top of the doors is also sometimes of this shape. It is of Indian origin, like all the rest of these details, and appears in China under the Sungs.[65] It is the pipal or lotus-headed window as found, for example, at Ajanta. There is also a new kind of curved tie-beam called lobster tie-beam *(ebi kōryō).* The ceilings are not coffered in the sanctuary, but flat, and no colored decoration is found as a rule. Most of these buildings have two-storied roofs and the bracketing is very profuse and complicated.

It is unfortunate that, though, through the importance of Zen Buddhism, the Kara style has had such a great influence on Japanese architecture, the Shariden or Relic Hall of the Engakuji is the only contemporary specimen left. As it persisted, however, later structures serve to illustrate its details.

In the Tenjiku style there are also certain peculiarities. The brackets have a round base like the *sarato* of the Asuka period, but of a different shape, and they also go through the pillars and project each side *(sashi-hijiki).* This arrangement allows the much deeper eaves to be supported more efficiently, for the long brackets are cantilevered on to beams inside the pillars. Here the ends of the rafters are not pointed or bevelled as in the Kara style, but blunt. There is also a new form of strut or king-post called *o-heisoku* or "big jar strut" from its shape. It is found in both these styles, more often in the Kara; but in the Tenjiku it is more cylindrical and should perhaps be called "round strut."

The famous Shariden of the Engakuji is all that is left of that temple, built by the Regent Hōjō Tokimune in 1283. It was made to house a relic presented by the Shogun Sanetomo, so it is said, and may have been later than the other buildings of the temple. It stands on a stone stylobate and the pillars have bases. It is 35 feet square and also 35 feet high. The bracketing of the lower story is simple enough, but that of the upper is rather complex, with close-bracketing on the plates that lie on the tops of the pillars. It has "fist nosing" at the end of these plates and the doors are of Chinese panelled style *(sankarado)* swinging on a pivot and not on hinges. The doors and windows have arched heads and the latter wooden lattices. The verge boards of the gable ends are also a new form called "double verges." The tie-beam used here is also different from those inside the building. It has an "eyebrow" on the lower edge and a "sleeve cutting" on both sides.

A new variety of building in the Kara style is the Founder's Hall (Kaisando) of the Eihōji temple at Toyooka village of the Kani district of Gifu prefecture. It was not built till 1352, apparently, and so does not come strictly into the Kamakura period, but it comes before the South and North dynasties were united, and this interval is sometimes reckoned as in the Kamakura rather than in the Muromachi period. It is a double structure arranged with an inner sanctuary and a prayer hall in front of it, the two connected by an antechamber. The front portion has a single roof and is with the antechamber on a lower level than the inner, which is reached by two steps. It has the complicated detail of the Kara style with close-bracketing of the triple type, whereas the inner sanctuary has a single roof of simple design with only one bracket in the center of the plate beside those over the four pillars. The roofs are of the hipped gable kind and of shingle, and they practically meet over the roof of the antechamber beneath, which is gabled. The whole arrangement and proportions of the shrine are very harmonious. If it were built with gable roofs it would be in the manner of the Hachiman shrine at Usa, but it is a much finer piece of work. It may owe something to this type but the plan was evidently an invention of this age and is, as before observed, the origin of the Gongen shrine. It is very pure Kara style and has elaborate ornamentation in the gable ends with a special type of verge-board and kingpost on the tie-beams. The curve of the roofs of each part of the building is different.

Turning to the Tenjiku style, the Nandaimon or Great South Gate of the Tōdaiji at Nana is a well-known example. It was rebuilt by the priest Shunjōbō Jōgen in 1199, with the Great Buddha Hall; but the latter was again burnt by Matsunaga Hisahide in the Oda period and so does not survive in its original state. It is 120 feet wide by 90 feet high with three gates 15 feet wide and 20 feet high—a huge and imposing structure with its mighty pillars each made of one great tree, and its forest of bracketing. The brackets are mortised right through these pillars and project in sextuple form some 15 feet to support the eaves in front, though they do not extend horizontally. They are cantilevered on to the cross-beams that hold the pillars together, as can be seen in the illustration (Plate 71). The bracket capitals have a moulded base of the *sarato* type. These capitals are placed so that the corner elbow goes across them diagonally, which is characteristic of this style. This gate has no ceiling and the pillars are visible right up to their tops. On these tops are great capitals on which the cross-beams rest, and on these are the frog-crotches of the Tenjiku style supporting a second set of tie-beams on which rest the supports of the roof.

The library of Kami Daigo is another specimen. It is a pyramidal building with the roof sloping down in front to cover with its eaves a porch that has a colonnade of four pillars. There is no ceiling inside, but the Sutra library stands under a gabled roof of its own with finely proportioned doors, the pivots of which are inserted in a circular fluted fitting applied to the lintel and called *waraza* (straw seat). The sets of tie-beams resting on the tops of the pillars themselves support tapering struts that hold up the roof. The pillars of this building appear at first sight to have a bulge, but actually only the upper portion of them tapers. It is a very neat and well-mannered building of pleasing proportions.

The belfry of the Tōdaiji seems to date from 1239, for on the sixth day of the sixth month of that year it is written in the temple archives that the bell fell down and was hung again in the tenth month. This rebuilding in four months seems very rapid, but is not impossible. On the boss of the bell is the inscription "Cast on the thirtieth day of the ninth month of the first year of Enō (1239) by the chief bell-founder Sahyoe-no-jō Nobutoki and twenty craftsmen." The belfry has a hipped gable roof with a sharp curve. The bell is hung from a great log under which are solid frog-crotches that rest on two other logs of the same size and these again are supported in the same way on the transverse beams. These beams project through the pillars and have ornamental ends in the Tenjiku manner.

The Composite Style

The Main Hall of the Kanshinji temple at Kawakami in the Minami Kawachi district of Osaka is the stock example of the mixture of the Kara style with the Wa or Japanese. It is about 65 feet square by 45 feet high and has a hipped gable roof. On top of the pillars it has the three branched brackets of the Wa style and between them the double ones of the Kara. The pillars are round with tapering tops, but those supporting the lean-to roof of the porch are square.

A distinctly peculiar building in the Japanese style that is one of the sights of Kyoto is the Sanju-sangen-do, which belongs to this period. The name means the Thirty-three-ken Hall. It was originally built by the Retired Emperor Go-Shirakawa beside his palace of the Hōjuji-den, but was destroyed and rebuilt in 1267. Actually it is not 33 *ken* long but 35, just as the Temple of Seven Halls has not actually that number, nor the Sammon three gates. Just how it got the name is unknown; but anyhow it is the longest of all temples, its measurement being 384 feet 6 inches, though it is only 5 *ken* or 30 feet deep. This shape was intended to accommodate the thousand and more images that it contains, but it was also most convenient for the Samurai archers who got into the habit of using its veranda as a shooting-range—for which it is very well suited. Possibly the name may have come from the range. Whatever the monks may have thought of this indignity, it is not on record that they protested.

The following is a plan of the way the styles mingled.

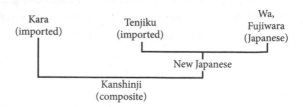

It is to be noted that the frog-crotches of this age are already elaborately decorated with openwork carving and the triangular brackets of the tail rafters (*tabasami)* are also carved in various patterns. The shrines of this period continue to be more and more influenced by

Buddhist architecture and now have pillars, bracketing, and roofs just like those of temples. The curved Chinese gable over the porch (*kara-hafu*), which has been used ever since, now first made its appearance, it seems, for there are not, in Professor Amanuma's opinion, any unchallenged examples before these days. The Mikumari shrine at Akasaka village in the South Kawachi district of Osaka has three separate shrines set side by side and connected by a corridor, which is unusual. Another well-known example is the Itsukushima shrine at Miyajima, one of the Three Sights of Japan, and situated conveniently on the tourist route on its island in the Inland Sea. It is said to date from the Suiko era, but Taira Kiyomori rebuilt it on its present plan when he was Governor of that district and made it a place of Imperial Pilgrimage, because he thought the favor of its Deity was the cause of his greatness. But it was burnt in 1225 and rebuilt in 1242. Then Mori Motonari, Lord of Choshu, remodelled it in 1558, and the only part that has survived from the Kamakura age is the Kyakuden or Guest-God's Shrine. It is built in the Shinden style like a palace by the sea, which flows under part of it at high tide, and its shingled roofs blend harmoniously with the green hills in the background. Its layout is somewhat unconventional to suit the peculiar situation. The Guest Shrine has Sanctuary (Honden), Hall of Offerings (Heiden), and other buildings one behind the other like a temple, and its architecture is that of the Fujiwara period in all respects.

Not much is known of the palace architecture of this age, except that toward the end of it there was no proper palace and the Emperor lived in Sato Dairi or Rural Palaces. Yoritomo had rebuilt the palace in Kyoto, but it was burnt in 1219. It was partially rebuilt and burnt again in 1227. Then Go Daigo Tenno began to rebuild it; but his days were short and it was never finished. The Southern Emperor had various residences while the Northern Sovereign lived in the Tsuchi Mikado mansion in Nishi-no-Dōin. Other Rural Palaces were the Saga and Fushimi mansions, in the latter of which lived the Retired Emperor Go Saga and the Emperors Go Fukakusa and Kameyama.

As Japan was now under the control of military magnates, it was natural that a type of residence suitable to their needs should develop. Not all the details of it are clear, but generally speaking it was a simple kind of house with a board roof and floors on which sitting cushions were used, and in some cases it was surrounded by a board fence and had earth-topped gates beside which were *yagura* or archers' towers for defence. The entrance was opposite the front gate and on the right was the *tosamurai* or apartment for the "outside retainers" who did not live inside. On the left of the entrance was a wide veranda with a Chinese gable in the middle of it and an ordinary one at the end. The inner rooms had alcoves and shelves and a *shōin*[66] a sort of reading alcove first found in this age and adopted from the Zen temple, and from which this kind of house came to be called Shōin style as distinguished from Shinden style, that of the court nobility. *Shōji* or papered sliding doors and wooden sliding doors were also used instead of the hinged *shitomi* of the Shinden mansion. There appears to have been a Spear Room, Head Inspection Room, Long Hearth Room, Reception Room, called Dei, Study, Official Document Room or Library (Kobunsho) and so on. Unlike the Shinden mansion it was all under one roof and not under several connected by corridors. But for lodging the retainers there may very likely have been other buildings.[67] Naturally no example of this kind of residence has survived; so what is known can only be deduced from descriptions in contemporary writings and to an extent from some plans of a later date, and quite possibly reproducing some later features such as the *tokonoma* and *chigaidana,* which were not yet known. There is, however, a reception room in the Kangakuin of the Enjōji temple at Otsu that has survived from this age. Grating windows were used in this period with wooden bars just like those in medieval Europe. They often formed a long continuous opening like a *ramma* (openwork frieze) above the ogee arched windows. These military residences were much like large farm-houses. The expression *Kita-no-kata* or Lady of the North for the wives of nobles or *Kita-no-Mandōkoro* (Government of the North) for those of Regents or Shoguns refers to the inner part of the house in which they lived, since these residences normally faced south.

CHAPTER 8

Muromachi Period (1340-1570 A.D.)

THE MUROMACHI period may be taken as from 1340 to 1570 or from the union of the North and South dynasties in 1394 to the end of the Genki era in 1573, about 230 years in the first case or 180 in the second.

No great innovation in architectural style took place in it, but the Kara style increased its popularity with that of the Zen sect and made its effects felt in other buildings beside temples. The other styles are found as well, however; but no very great architectural masterpiece has survived from this age, in which the examples of the Kara style are inferior to those of the preceding one. Again, unfortunately more than half of the temples in Kyoto, the capital of the Ashikaga Shoguns who removed it back again from Kamakura, were destroyed in the civil wars of the Onin period (1460-). Architecture ran to elegance and delicacy rather than to grandeur—in which it was very representative of the age and the rulers, for the Ashikaga Shoguns were, with the exception of the first, luxurious and fastidious aesthetes who became more and more involved in the bonds of ceremony and convention. Consequently the Empire was never properly under their control and eventually they lost the little power they had and those feudal wars ensued which were so damaging to buildings.

The most prominent works of the period are residences rather than temples, for it became the fashion to build fine mansions in carefully planned landscape gardens, and the characteristic Japanese arts of garden-planning, tea-ism, and flower arrangement as we know them, now arose under the Ashikagas to vigorous growth, though the germ had been there for a long time.

There is a big stupa-shaped pagoda at the Dai-dempōin at Negoro, the branch monastery of the Shingon monks of Mount Koya, rebuilt in 1516, that luckily survived Hideyoshi's burning of some of the buildings in 1586. It is the largest specimen of this type and must be much like the original at Koya which now no longer exists.

Also in the village of Bessho, in the Chiisagata district of Nagano at the Anrakuji temple, is the only remaining example of an octagonal pagoda in Japan. This is the common form in China, and small ones of stone are to be seen in Japan too. There was a nine-storied specimen of very large dimensions at the Hoshōji temple at Kyoto according to tradition, but it is there no longer. This one is three-storied, with another set of eaves below that makes it look four-storied; or perhaps it was intended to have four stories, as an exception to the rule that pagodas have always an odd number of stories. For Japanese dislike even asymmetry unalloyed. It is 40 feet high and the *sōrin* (spire) of cast iron is 20 feet high. The first two stories are noticeably closer to each other than those above them and Professor Amanuma observes that this is rather a feature of Zen buildings. The style is strongly Kara with some modifications in the detail.

The Kinkaku of the Kaenji, or Golden Pavilion, which is so well known as to be a bit hackneyed, was begun in 1398 by the Shogun Ashikaga Yoshimitsu on the site of a villa belonging to the Saionji lord of that day, Kintsune by name. It was called the North Hill Mansion (Kitayama Dono); but after his death he left it to be turned into a temple. This Golden Pavilion is the only survivor of many buildings which have all disappeared. It is a blend of residence and temple. This three-storied pavilion in a landscape garden is a new form of palatial residence produced by the ways of the age.

Yoshimitsu's villa had thirteen buildings in all. The Shishinden, an imitation of that in the Imperial Palace, which was definitely presumptuous for a subject, the Hall of the Court Nobles, the Pavilion of the Mirror of Heaven (Tenkyo-kaku), the Hall of the Confession of the Doctrine (Gehōdo), the North-Gazing Hall (Kyōboku-do), the Snow-Viewing Arbor (Kansetsu-tei), the Relic Hall (Shariden), the Hall of the Waters (Izumi-dono), the Hall of Fragrant Virtue (Hōtokuden), the Lesser Hall (Komi-do), the Jizo Hall (Jizo-do), and others beside an arched bridge (Sori-bashi). The Shishinden was of the eight-gabled type that originated in the Kamakura era with a throne in the middle and eight dragons in gold lacquer on the roof, if the descriptions are to be credited. The Kinkaku itself was originally on an island in the lake and approached by the large arched bridge from the Hall of Fragrant Virtue, as seems very suitable. The Ginkaku had twelve buildings, among them a Hall of the Waters called Pure Diversion Arbor (Rōsei-tei), a room constructed on a boat on the lake called Night-moored Ship (Yōhaku-sen), a roofed bridge called Dragon's Back Bridge (Ryūse-kyo), besides a Great Shōin, an Entrance Hall, and, not least, a bathroom.

The room on a boat is a device sometimes seen in modern residences and restaurants, and a very pleasing one in hot weather. Sometimes there is no lake but only one of those skilfully arranged groupings of rocks and water-plants that produce a vivid illusion of one.

When these Shoguns retired from the cares of office, such as it was, and which they were not slow to quit, they became Zen monks after the style of Retired Emperors, and since they lived in the Imperial Capital and not a military one like the lords of Kamakura or Edo, the imitation was the more natural. Actually their dress and the ecclesiastical touches in the architecture of their mansions were about the only monastic aspects of their life.

The first two stories of the Kinkaku are the same size, 30 feet by 24 feet, and there is a porch projecting from the ground floor. They are called Hōsui-in (Hall of the Water of Doctrine) and Chōōnkaku (Pavilion of the Sound of the Tide) respectively. The third story, called Kyukeicho (Carefully-finished Top), is about 18 feet square and has a pyramidal roof with a nectar-pot finial on which is a jewel-shaped boss surmounted by a phoenix of gilt bronze. The two lower stories are in the Wa (Japanese) style with *shitomi* lattices and Chinese pivoted doors *(ita-karado)*. Both have verandas round them and outer balconies, that on the second story being supported by bracketing. The upper story has Chinese panelled doors *(San-Karado)* with ogee arch windows and lotus ornamented balcony rail in Kara style. The two lower stories were decorated in colors over black lacquer while the third was covered with gold leaf both within and without, hence the name given to the whole. Professor Amanuma gives the proportions of the first and second stories as, Wa style 7/10, Kara 1/5, Tenjiku 1/10; and of the upper story as Kara 9/10. The effect of this pavilion is somewhat reminiscent of Akbar's marble Panch Mahall at Fatehpur Sikri, though this is a three- and not a five-storied Vihara.

The Ginkaku or Silver Pavilion of the Gishōji is of the same kind but smaller and two-storied, while its details conform to the Shōin style rather than the Shinden. It also is the only survivor of a much more extensive establishment, for Ashikaga Yoshimasa began to build himself a villa here when the Onin war of 1468 interrupted his operations, and it was not till 1480 that he took up his residence again after his retirement and resumed them; but the building was not finished when he died seven years after.

The lower story is 23 by 18 feet and the upper is 18 feet square, very modest dimensions indeed. The roof is like that of the Kinkaku and the intention was to finish it with a covering of silver leaf, but this was never done and it is silver only by courtesy. The style is much the same as the other too, but the lower story has a flat boarded ceiling and waist-high *shōji* (*kōshi-shōji*) with sliding wooden doors, approaching very nearly to the modern Japanese interior. The upper story has three arched windows in front and two, with a pair of panelled doors, on the opposite side; this is repeated on the two other sides.

Attached to the same temple of Gishōji is the Tōkyudo. Yoshimasa's private Buddhist chapel with a tearoom of four and a half mats, the first to be constructed in Japan.[68] It measures 30 by 24 feet and is 22 feet high, with a shingled hipped gable roof and a veranda round it. This also has waist-high *shōji* and boarded floor. The Buddhist shrine of Amida has a coved ceiling and Chinese panelled doors on pivots with a board floor, while the tearoom floor is covered with the four mats and a half that was to become the normal size for this kind of chamber. It has a board ceiling, a built-out writing alcove (*tsuke-shōin*), and a chigaidana or set of shelves. Here too there are waist-high *shōji* and *mairado* or ribbed wooden sliding doors.

The shrines of the Muromachi era again became more and more like Buddhist temples with double hipped gable roofs and elaborate carvings, so that it is very difficult at times to distinguish between the two. The Kibitsu shrine at Ichinomiya in the Kibi district of Bizen province is an ancient one said to date from the days of the Emperor

Nintoku, A.D. 313; but the present structure was rebuilt by Ashikaga Yoshimitsu in 1390 and is a very complicated building. The roof is shingled and has double gables over the hip of the *irimoya,* while the oratory or Haiden is built on in front like a vestibule. Inside the floor rises in stages and the ceiling with it, which gives a somewhat uncommon effect. The pillars carry *sashi-hijiki* or traversing brackets in the Tenjiku style. The oratory is also two-storied, but the lower story has a tiled roof like that of a veranda and over this a range of lattice windows, a feature very rarely found. It has also the "lobster" tiebeams and jar-shaped king-posts of the Kara style. The outside of the roof has the typical Shinto cross-beam construction, but only applied and loosely connected with the ridge, looking like an afterthought.

This age was not an auspicious one for the Imperial Palace and its occupants. It was burnt several times and the Northern Emperor set up by the Ashikaga Shogun lived in the Tsuchi-mikado Detached Palace. It was burnt in the Onin civil wars and the Emperor escaped the fire with difficulty. Then, in 1473, attempts were made to rebuild it on a much smaller scale, but the country was distracted by feudal wars and the Imperial Domains were lost so that the Throne had no funds and had to depend on contributions from some loyal feudal lords. The great Court festivals could no longer be observed, for there were no proper buildings in which to hold them. Even the Senyōden where the Sacred Mirror was kept was in ruins.

The feudal lords, however, like the Shogun, had a tradition of magnificence, and in the latter days of the Ashikaga house the great lords were more wealthy and secure than the Shogun. None of their mansions have survived, but the descriptions of the Flower Palace of Yoshimitsu at Muromachi show that it was a mixture of Shōin and Shinden styles, a blending of the Court style with the military residence. It had an entrance hall, Shinden and Shōin halls and *tai* or connected wings. But the mansions of Yoshimasa and Yoshinao were entirely in the Shōin style.

The word *shōin* means "study" and it was taken from the architecture of the Zen temple imported from India via China. In the temple it was the name of the library, for it literally means writing or book room; but when the military class became so much given to Zen they made such a room in their residences, where they could read Chinese texts (for the Zen monks taught the Confucian classics also) or meditate if so inclined. And as they came to receive guests there the reception room acquired the name Shōin. The inner part of it was raised as a dais *(jōdan* or upper step) on which the lord sat. Behind this was the *tokonoma* or alcove and the *chigaidana* or asymmetric shelves, a variety of built-in sideboard. The rooms were divided from one another by *fusuma* and closed in on the outside by *shōji;* but *amado,* or outside wooden rain-doors sliding on the edge of the veranda, were not introduced till the Momoyama age and then were not universal.

The word *genkan* or entrance hall (dark space) was another expression borrowed from the Zen monastery and is now the ordinary word for this part of a Japanese house, while in these days the word *shōin* is still used to mean the built-in writing table with small *shōji* behind it, which is often found beside the *tokonoma* in reception rooms of the better kind. The decoration of the interior of these rooms was confined to black-and-white sketches on the walls and *fusuma.* The wood was plain but might be lacquered black in some cases.

After the Genkan or porch was attached to the house the chamber within was enlarged and became the place where the Samurai retainers hung up their weapons and which they used as a guard-room. So its name became changed from Hiro-hisashi (wide veranda) of the Shinden style to Hiroma or Great Hall of the Shōin, and the Tozamurai of the older military residence was no longer needed or provided.

The Ashikaga house had *shitomi* and *yarido* (suspended grating windows and sliding doors) and a Tozamurai (guard-house). The floors were all boarded and had loose *tatami* (mats) that were moved about where they were needed; but the floors were not yet covered entirely with them.

In the temple buildings there is a great increase of carving everywhere, on the beam-ends, frog-crotches, verges, and openwork friezes over the lintels *(ramma).* And the bracket capitals, too, become ornamented and foliate—the beginning of the debased forms they assumed in later days. On the other hand the influence of the Zen simplicity had banished the red and other colored decoration, and plain wood became the rule both inside and out.

Kō-no-Moronao (d.1351) said that ordinary Samurai below the fourth rank should not have boarded roofs of the kind called *seki-itauchi,* or even *noshi-buki.* They must have ordinary thatched roofs like those of farm-houses. The first kind is the more elaborate, made of overlapping boards with longitudinal braces to keep them in place; and the *noshi* roof is made of layers of thin boards held down by diagonal cross-pieces over which stones are laid to prevent the wind dislodging them. These roofs are common in the Hokuriku district in the north still.

The Daimyo Otomo in the fifteenth century lived in a thatched house with no *tatami.* If all lords had been like him the land would have been at peace, observes the chronicle.

In the Muromachi period even Samurai did not have a house with a large Shōin style room, much less the ordinary people. And most of the floors were of boards without *tatami.* The large boarded spaces in farmhouses are a survival of this. They are like those in the refectory of a temple.

The *tokonoma,* now a deep alcove in which pictures or scrolls of writing are hung and flower arrangements placed, always found in a reception room and in tearooms also, probably developed out of the Zen shrine which consisted of a picture of Buddha or Daruma hung on the wall with a small oblong table standing before it to hold a candlestick, flower vase, and censer. This table was called *oshi-ita* and was used in rooms of the Ashikaga time, but when it became a fixture it developed into the *tokonoma.* Even now a detachable stand of this kind is used in rooms that are too small for a normal *tokonoma,* the size of which must be in proportion to that of the room.

The *chigaidana* was probably a built-in version of the cabinet with similar shelves used in the Fujiwara Shinden mansion, though some say that these shelves were first used in the military residence and were put there for the heads taken by the warrior, the different levels in this case being explained as intended to correspond with the rank of the deceased and pay proper respect where it was due.

CHAPTER 9

Momoyama Period (1570-1616 A.D.)

THE Momoyama period is a short one of only forty years or so; but for activity it has been described as one in which every decade was equal to a century in most others, and as usual its architecture reflected its exceedingly vigorous life. This era saw the country united under one central administration by Nobunaga and Hideyoshi, those two remarkable characters who brought out of confusion and civil wars the beginning of the modern Japanese Empire. But, though rulers, they could not become Shogun, for neither happened to be of the Minamoto family from which alone convention decreed that Shoguns could be taken. Hideyoshi indeed was of no family at all. Nobunaga was one of the few Japanese autocrats to be assassinated when a little under fifty, and Hideyoshi died in 1598, whereupon their work was carried on by a third even more remarkable figure who was a Minamoto and therefore could and did become Shogun and the Divine Ancestor of a line of fifteen successors in that office. Though the Momoyama period actually ceased at the fall of the Toyotomis, the family of Hideyoshi, its atmosphere in architectural matters extended right on into the next period of the Tokugawa Shoguns, more or less till the end of the seventeenth century.

The speciality of this age was not so much religious edifices as palatial residences, military mansions, and castles, or perhaps the *simplex munditiis* of tearooms. As in the previous years the Wa, Kara, Tenjiku, and Composite styles continued to flourish and in details grew rather more ornate than ever. But though this was so the adventurous spirit of the time led it to the limit in experiments within these boundaries. And these experiments lay mostly in the sphere of painted and carved decoration of every sort, for great strides had been made in these arts of late and there were many great artists, craftsmen, and aesthetes ready to serve these brilliant and stimulating autocrats, of whom the first two, Nobunaga and Hideyoshi, were themselves exceedingly enthusiastic connoisseurs of all that was beautiful and uncommon. This is well seen in the two palatial mansions that they built, the Azuchi castle of Nobunaga and the Fushimi-Momoyama castle of Hideyoshi from which the period is named, not to mention Hideyoshi's Juraku mansion in Kyoto and his castle of Osaka. A bit vulgar and blatant it all may have seemed to the more subdued taste of the century before, but its colorful vigor was natural and characteristic, especially of a parvenu like Hideyoshi. For though some of the details were overloaded and some of the ornament useless, the architecture remained on the whole healthy, and real degeneration did not set in until the later period of Edo.

It was hardly to be expected that temple building would flourish under Nobunaga, for he hated the political activities of such sects as the Monto Amida Buddhists and Nichiren monks, which were rather pronounced in his day. And what Nobunaga disliked he had a habit of burning if he could. So that the destruction of religious buildings and their occupants under his rule was considerable. He saw in them an obstacle to his plan of establishing a central government for Japan. So did Hideyoshi in some cases, but he has been described as one whose speciality was water rather than fire and he preferred to flood out his enemies, a process that was not so destructive. Hideyoshi was by nature far the less drastic of the two and preferred to use temples for advertising himself, creating employment and popularity and making other people spend money.

Another phenomenon peculiar to this age was the appearance of Christian edifices like the colleges at Azuchi and Arima—groups of buildings in the Spanish or Italian style with chapel and campanile complete, as can be seen from the one or two rare illustrations that have survived. There was a big church in Kyoto called the Eirokuji or Temple of the Eiroku Era, from the date of its construction, but apparently better known to everybody as the Nambanji or Temple of Southern Barbarians. The interior is said to have been in European style, but some consider that the outside was not; and certainly a few rare screen pictures of the activities of the Portuguese at Nagasaki show what seem to be Christian churches in Japanese style, built like temples with a tower like a stupa pagoda, but with a cross on the top in place of the usual Buddhist finial. Oddly enough Nobunaga encouraged all this, not out of any liking for Christianity itself, for he was a rationalist, but because he hoped to see the political variety of it damage the same kind of Buddhism. Partly, too, because the missionaries brought him novelties which he appreciated, and had knowledge he could acquire. So it flourished all his days, but after his untimely death in 1582 Hideyoshi became suspicious of the Europeans, and started those repressive measures which continued under the Tokugawas and ended in the closing of the country and the very thorough destruction of everything suggestive of Christianity, even to the use of the date A.D.

But Hideyoshi favoured Buddhism to the extent that he liked to use it to glorify himself as well as to assist him politically. Thus he determined to build the biggest Buddha ever known, 160 feet high, and a temple 200 feet high to house it. This was the Hōkōji, intended to put the Great Buddha Hall of Nara in the shade. It was built in 1587, but destroyed in the great earthquake of 1612 and rebuilt again by his son Hideyori, on a smaller scale, with a 63-foot Buddha and a 160-foot temple. This was again destroyed in another earthquake and fire in 1798, and the present edifice that takes its place beside the Toyokuni shrine of Hideyoshi is very small indeed. This temple had a strangely political career, for when Hideyoshi built it he ordered the people to contribute their weapons for its metal work, thus disarming them, and literally forging their arms into hinges for the doors of the temple of the peaceful one to turn on. After its destruction Tokugawa Ieyasu, even more cunning than Hideyoshi, persuaded his son Hideyori to spend any amount of money in rebuilding it so that he might not have the wherewithal to buy armaments. Finally, when it was rebuilt, Ieyasu, who had repudiated with indignation the suggestion that he should contribute something to it, made the inscription on its great bell a pretext to start a war with Hideyori and eventually destroy him. It was in some sort an epitome of the methods of those interesting times. The plan that has survived from about 1700 shows that it was just the same type as the Nara Daibutsu-den built in the Tenjiku style with septuple bracketing, the largest number used. It had 92 pillars from 5 to 5½ feet in diameter, or, according to Amanuma, 88. It was supported by four huge tie-beams connecting the four pillars that surrounded the space where the image was placed, just like the 78-foot beams (13-*ken* beams) of the present-day Tōdaiji Daibutsu-den. The dimensions given on the plan are 110 feet long by 70 feet deep.

The Kyō-ō Gōkokuji or Tōji is another building with a mixture of styles, for it has Tenjiku pillars and brackets with a Wa style quadrangle and bracketing in the upper story, while the shape of the brackets throughout is of the Wa type.

The kitchen and refectory *(Kuri)* of the Myōshinji is a fine specimen of the work of this age. Tradition says it was built by Hideyoshi when he fed a thousand monks, and the date 1605 is on the end tile of one of the gabled smoke-vents. It is 74 feet long by 78 feet deep and 51 feet high to the roof ridge. It has a Chinese gable over the entrance and all the details, frog-crotches, verges, tie-beams, and beam-ends are elaborately carved, and the *omoto* or *Rhodea japonica* appears here as a decoration for the first time. There are two gabled smoke-vents on the high roof, the eaves of which roof come down to within 21 feet of the ground. One part of the interior is covered with mats and with the exception of the earthen part the rest is floored with boards. The ceiling is what is called *no-tenjo,* i.e. one that has the beams covered in with ordinary boards like an outhouse. As a temple refectory this one is certainly out of the ordinary.

The Kōdaiji was built by Kōdaiin the wife of Hideyoshi (posthumous name) as a mausoleum for him in 1606. The pillars and doors and other fittings are all finished in what is known as Kōdaiin lacquer and the ceilings of the Kaisando or Founder's Hall are made from the wood of a warship that Hideyoshi used in the Korean campaign and from his wife's palanquin. Some of the finest lacquer work of the time was designed by Hon-ami Kō-etsu and known by his name. Its merit lay in taste and design rather than any technique, and it is very often done on a background of plain wood. In the Kōdaiji is the tearoom that Hideyoshi used, and there is another in the Hiunkaku, his villa.

The Daigo Samboin at Yamashina is a temple that Hideyoshi restored to use for a flower-viewing festival. The buildings are a mixture of a Shinden with a tiled roof and a Shōin with a thatched one. The garden Hideyoshi designed himself, as he also supervised the restoration of the rooms, for which, as usual, he used material taken from other temples.

Two new forms of shrines appear about this time, namely the Gongen type and a modification of it called the Eight-roofed style (Yatsu-mune-zukuri). The Gongen style derives from the Eihōji temple with its oratory and sanctuary joined by a connecting chamber. When this middle chamber is on the same level as the oratory it is called Heiden or Hall of Offerings, but when it is lower, as in the Eihōji, and paved with stone it is called the Stone Chamber (Ishi-noma) as it is at the Nikko Tōshōgu. Then two wings are pushed out from the oratory and a lean-to attached to the sanctuary, producing a fairly complicated roof called the Eight-roofed type, though the actual number is not so many. The only shrine that has its full complement is the well-known Tenjin shrine at Kitano in Kyoto, built in 1608—and that has really only seven. It is the first shrine to have a Stone Hall. It has a Chinese gable over the porch and a *chidori*[69] gable in the roof over it—which is quite superfluous and in poor taste, for it does nothing but look expensive. This shrine is a good example of the extent to which Shinto had been absorbed, externally, by Buddhist architecture.

The same thing happened to the Imperial Palaces which were again rebuilt first by Nobunaga and then by Hideyoshi and Ieyasu. The Shishinden and Seiryoden and Senyoden and the other buildings rose again, but with the original Shinden style was now mingled the Buddhist that was so pervasive. When they were again restored and largely reconstructed in the Kanei era (1624-41) by Tokugawa Iemitsu, several of the buildings were presented to various temples and re-erected, so that they can still be seen. One of these is the Imperial Envoy's Gate of the Daitokuji Zen monastery at Kyoto. It was once the south gate of the palace as rebuilt by Hideyoshi in 1591, and was transported here in 1641. It is largely in the Kara style, a very graceful though elaborately decorated structure. Part of the Katsura Detached Palace, a very famous building, is of this age also, for the Shōin and Gepparo pavilions were built by Hideyoshi for Prince Tomohito, adopted son of the Emperor Ogimachi. The rest of it and the garden were the work of Kobori Enshu when he was Commissioner for Fushimi. It is a very simple set of thatched buildings arranged *en échelon* from the Shōin to the Miyuki Goten and "looking when viewed from the garden rather like a house-boat." This view from the garden is most elegant and, though very simple, the villa has infinite variety in its construction and all the details are uncommon. Naturally it is much imbued with the Chanoyu feeling.[70]

The same process of removal to temples has fortunately preserved some splendid examples of mansions of the Momoyama age. There are the remains of Hideyoshi's Jurakutei mansion and the Hiunkaku lake villa now in the grounds of the Nishi Hongwanji monastery, where they were sent by Iemitsu, and the Great Shōin or Hall of Audience at the same temple with the Noh stage, the adjoining reception rooms and the Imperial Envoy's Gate (Chokushi-mon) all from his mansion at Fushimi. These represent the full flower of the Shōin style with dais at the upper end and a rather shallow *tokonoma,* the wall behind decorated with paintings on a ground of gold like the *fusuma* that divide the rooms, and the friezes (*ramma*) profusely carved in openwork. Beside the dais are four doors above a deep sill that is lacquered black like those of the dais and *tokonoma.* These doors open on to the Tonomo or Guard Chamber where the armed retainers stood unseen, ready for any emergency. They also are painted and have heavy tasselled cords to draw them back instead of the usual sunk pushes or *hikite* which are normally found. Next to it is the ante-chamber and then the third chamber divided off by painted *fusuma.* The rooms have *shōji* with *mairado* or wooden doors outside them. Beyond them is the wide matted veranda or corridor called *irikawa* and beyond that again the narrower wood-floored one. Later on *amado* or outside shutters were fitted on the outer edge of this, making the *mairado* unnecessary. The Great Gate, of the "four-legged" variety, (Yotsu-ashi-mon) is a massive and imposing structure most elaborately carved, though without impairing its constructive qualities or giving it the overloaded effect of the Nikko gates. More delicate and not so heavily ornate is the Karamon or Chinese Gate of the Daitokuji monastery that came from the Jūraku mansion. It is 30 feet high and 33 feet wide with Chinese gables on each side, making it 25 feet deep. The gates have fine metal mounts, the beams are carved with fish in waves, dragons, and lions, and the ends of the gables filled in with openwork carvings of birds and pine-trees.

The Great Hall of the Hongwanji is 207.3 feet long and 92.2 feet wide. It may be divided into two parts. The Great Hall of Audience, called Kō-no-ma or Crane Chamber because the *ramma* are carved with these birds with backgrounds of reeds and clouds, is said to be the work of Hidari Jingoro, the Grinling Gibbons of Japan. The *tokonoma* has a projecting Shōin with a large ornamental window, and the ceiling, which is a coved coffered one over the dais and a flat coffered one elsewhere, has paintings of birds and flowers, dragons and the like in the coffers. The *fusuma* and the walls and lower parts of the waist-high *shōji* are all painted with designs on a gold ground—Chinese scenes on the dais and flowers and birds elsewhere, mostly by Kano Tannyu. Behind the *tokonoma* is a scene with the Emperor Wu and the goddess Si Wang Mu which is characteristic, for these Japanese autocrats liked pictures of Chinese Court scenes, especially those of the great Empire of T'ang, just as Napoleon and others liked to recall ancient Rome. It is to be noted that the doors of the Tonomo here are in line with the *tokonoma* and not at right angles to it as elsewhere. Behind these spacious rooms is a smaller set called the White Shōin, also with dais reception room decorated in the same way with second and third chambers in front of it. The Dais Room has also a dressing-room in its rear. Parallel with these and the Great Reception Room on the left are another series of rooms, the Chrysanthemum and Wild-goose chambers with an *irikawa* and an antechamber, beside which is the entrance hall with another antechamber. On the right side is a third *irikawa* and three more rooms, the Drum Room (Taikono-ma) and the Wave Room (Nami-no-ma), named as usual from the subject of the decoration and as richly ornamented as the rest.

Hideyoshi's lake villa, the Hiunkaku or Flying Cloud Pavilion, rises in three stories of different sizes something like a very exaggerated version of the Ginkakuji. The lower story has two main rooms: the reception room called Shokenden (Hall Inviting Discrimination) with dais and projecting Shōin windows; it is sometimes called the Willow Chamber because it is decorated with willows under snow by Kano Eitoku. Next to it is the antechamber and then the Embarking Chamber, with steps leading down to a landing stage from which to enter a boat. The second story has also Jōdan and Gedan, dais and lower room, and the papered ceiling of the Jōdan is decorated with paintings by Kano Sanraku, while there are also pictures of the Six Poets after which it is named. This story has a balcony round it. The third story, called Plucking Star Pavilion (Tekiseirō), is quite small and has ornamental windows shaped like a war fan. The roofs are all of shingle and comprise all shapes, hipped gable, Chinese gable, ordinary gable, and pyramidal. The timbers with which is it built are all quite light and slender and unadorned, and its recherche but simple elegance shows the influence of the Chanoyu feeling very strongly, as might be expected of any one so devoted to it as Hideyoshi and such a friend of the first of Tea-masters, Sen Rikyu.

Attached to the Hiunkaku by a covered way is the bathroom, called Kikakudai[71] or Yellow Crane Terrace. It measures 66 by 24 feet, and consists of a single-storied building with a shingled pyramidal roof in which is a sitting-room with a balcony looking over the lake, attached to another on a lower level with a gabled roof for the dressing-room, next to which comes the bathroom itself on a lower level still. The bath is a steam chamber with a Chinese gabled roof, and the sitting-room is decorated with convolvulus by Kano Eitoku. The end of the sixteenth century was not, I imagine, except perhaps in India, Turkey, or Cairo, a period when bathrooms, elegant or otherwise, were very common; so that this one, built as it is entirely of wood, is the more noteworthy. There is also a tearoom attached to the villa, which, it is perhaps unnecessary to say, is perfectly well suited in every way for modern living conditions.

Up to this time there had not been in Japan anything that could properly be called a castle. There were only hills and other strategic places defended by moats, natural or artificial, earthworks, and stockades. These were effective enough for their purpose, which was the protection of the lord's residence against sudden raids or the holding of an important place for a time by a garrison, as block-houses on a provincial frontier. But the Japanese Samurai did not fancy the defensive much and usually preferred to use these forts as places from which he could sally out to the attack. The feudal lords depended on their field army and knew better than to be cooped up in places where it might be surrounded. And it was said of Takeda Shingen, one of the greatest strategists of the day, that he never built any strong place. This was partly, no doubt, because his provinces of Kai and Shinano were exceedingly mountainous and he could hold them very well as they were. And the nature of the country with its narrow roads and gorges between hills and its stretches of flooded ricefields on the flat, intersected only by narrow paths, meant that it was to a large extent a natural fortress and little more was needed. The strongest places were such sites as that of Osaka—which the Hongwanji monks held against Nobunaga for seven years, and even then they were only persuaded to get out by Imperial Edict. This was so surrounded by rivers as to form natural moats almost all round it, one of them being wide enough to make it easy to get provisions without interference from the besiegers.

However the introduction of firearms made it advisable, perhaps under the influence of European fortress plans, possibly supplied by the Portugese, to proceed to heavier fortifications and crenellated walls and towers. Firearms and Christianity entered Japan at almost the same time and in the same place, somewhere about 1540 and in the province of Satsuma in the island of Kyushu, the Daimiate of the house of Shimazu, the most ancient of the families of military aris-tocrats in Japan. Thus if, as some aver, the Jesuits gave Nobunaga the plans of the first castle, the antidote was supplied by the Portuguese as well as the poison—somewhat as they seem to have supplied the first public hospitals, after they had brought syphilis to fill them.

They were, as a Japanese historian comments, then a very energetic people. But the Japanese themselves were no less so, for the castles they forthwith proceeded to build were extremely imposing looking piles, with their lofty many-gabled keeps rising story over story in the main ward and surrounded by heavily walled second and third wards with lofty towers and massive loopholed gates. They look bigger as a rule than their European prototypes and certainly handsomer, but they are not so consistently massively built, since their upper structures of walls and towers were made only of wood and plaster. The great ramparts beneath, however, lack nothing of solidity, and the moats were generally some 60 or 70 feet wide. But though they look formidable enough few of them were ever used, for they were built after the country had been unified and pacified by Hideyoshi and further consolidated by Ieyasu. Hideyori did sustain a siege in the greatest of them outside of Edo, the castle of Osaka, but it was taken more by intrigue than by assault, and practically all the fighting took place outside it. Therefore the historian Tokutomi is not far wrong in calling these castles "'great advertisement towers,'" very typical of a flamboyant age that liked to make a fine show.

The first of these castles was built by Nobunaga in 1576[72] on Azuchi Hill, which projects into a lagoon formed by two islands between two long promontories, thus making it into a natural moat round the hill on three sides. Nothing of it now remains but the foundation stones, for it was burnt soon after its lord's death. It was a mixture of fortress and residence with a seven-storied keep called Tenshu, a word first found in this period, and first applied to the keep of a castle at Itami. It is equivalent to Teishakuten or the Heaven of Brahma, the highest of the thirty-three Heavens of Mount Sumeru, which according to Buddhist pictures rises in tiers like a huge wedding-cake, and has nothing to do with Christianity as sometimes alleged. This keep has its architectural prototype in the Kinkakuji and Ginkakuji pavilions of the Ashikagas, of which Hideyoshi's Hiunkaku is a further development. It was situated in the Hon Maru or main ward, the wards of a Japanese castle being called Kuruwa or Maru, both words meaning round. There were also Ni-no-maru and San-no-maru, second and third wards. Round the main castle were the fortified mansions of the great lords, his vassals and allies. The keep stood on a stone foundation 70 feet high and was of seven stories, rising over a 100 feet more.

Nobunaga's secretary has left a careful description of the interior which he says contained forty-five rooms and a landscape garden 72 feet long on the fourth story, with rocks and trees. On this story, too, was a place for playing hand-ball. The sixth story had an octagonal room with an area of 24 square feet of which the inner pillars were lacquered red and the outer ones gilt. One reception room was covered with linen lacquered black and another was all gilt without any other decoration at all, but very many were painted with such subjects as the Confucian sages, Buddha preaching to his disciples, Taoist Rishi and the more usual bird and flower, bamboo and pine motifs. It was "a splendid residence with superb views from the various apartments over the lake and its islands, to the distant hills beyond with the villages nestling in the plain between, and from the temple of Chōmyoji the sound of the evening bell came echoing over the water." A very suitable dwelling for a martial aesthete and at the same time a demonstration to the whole country that here, surrounded by the mighty, he ruled it.

It is said that the keep of Azuchi[73] was sharp at the top and looked like a Siamese pagoda, and it is suggested that this may have been due to a Portuguese strain introduced by Nobunaga's missionary acquaintances. There is no knowing what he might have done, and at any rate he wore a black Portuguese hat and had a negro servant. Some of the material for this castle he took from the Nijo palace which he had built for the Shogun Ashikaga Yoshiaki. For when he deposed him it stood empty and Nobunaga resumed about half of it, and this palace itself was constructed of materials appropriated from various temples in Kyoto. Japanese architecture is as adaptable as the people themselves and the withdrawal of comparatively few mortises will turn a temple into a mansion and vice versa. The tiles of the Azuchi keep were also said to have been gilt up to the fifth story, and fragments of tiles of this kind have been turned up on the site.

Hideyoshi's great castle of Osaka was built in 1584 on the site of Ishiyama, the fortified position held by the Hongwanji monks and which Nobunaga had no time to deal with after he took it. It was an even better place than Azuchi, with rivers on three sides and the river Yodo giving access to the sea. Inside this two more concentric moats were made. Nothing now remains of the castle, which had a five-storied keep and was about seven miles in circumference, for it was burnt and never rebuilt. There was the Hon-maru, Ni-no-maru, Yamasato-maru, and San-no-maru, four wards in all. Hideyoshi requisitioned materials and labor from all the Daimyos of western Japan to construct it, and the size of some of the stones is remarkable. Several used in the gates measure 9 by 18 feet, and there is another 25 feet long, reaching from the base of the gate to the bottom of the lower story of the tower above. The gates of these castles were surrounded by massive stone walls like a box—hence the name for them, "Masugata" or "rice measure." Those entering were faced by a blank wall opposite, and the exit was through the side wall at right angles to it. Above these walls were works from which missiles could be shot from all sides into the enclosure as well as in front of it. Sometimes there was a barbican (*de-maru* or projecting ward), as at Osaka where it was called Sanada-maru after the designer Sanada Yukimura—one of the greatest experts in fortification of the day, who defended Osaka against Ieyasu and fell with it.

Other notable castles that belong to this age are Himeji, Okayama, Hiroshima, and Hikone, the last being remarkable for its balcony and ornamental ogee windows in the upper story like the Kinkakuji, Kagoshima, Kumamoto, Wakamatsu, Nagoya, Matsuyama, Matsue, Fukuoka, and some others. Edo castle also, the largest of all, was already being built and was of the same type. The building of this and many of the castles above mentioned almost simultaneously, in the early years of the seventeenth century, was one of the ways employed by Ieyatsu to empty the pockets of the Daimyos and render them innocuous. For a castle was not built by the owner alone; his neighbors were all involved. These great castles were those of the lords of a whole province but there were lesser ones belonging to

Daimyos who had only part of a province and who were therefore known as Castle Lords. Those who could not afford a castle had a fortified mansion and were known as Territorial Lords.

The styles in this period are all mixed and the details highly ornate so that in many cases this quality obscures the functional use of the elements. The tie-beams and beam-ends are richly carved often so that they lose their constructive shape. The beam-ends become more realistically elephant-headed and less suggestive than before, from the influence of the Kara style, and are often put where they are not needed merely as an extra decoration. The frog-crotches are carved in openwork as a rule, and are often weak looking in the legs and not very functional, for they do not look equal to supporting the weight above them. They often have a bracket capital on top that holds an elbow over it and this in turn supports the beam. The king-posts, too, are over-ornamented and sometimes introduced where unnecessary. The same may be said of the rafter brackets (tabasami). They are beautifully carved with flowers and angels in clouds and so on, but they seem to cling precariously to the rafters rather than hold them up.

CHAPTER 10

Edo Period (1616-1860 A.D.)

THE early part of the Edo era does not differ much in its architecture from the Momoyama period, since those craftsmen and artisans who had worked for the Toyotomis continued to work for the Tokugawas. So things went on without much change till about 1700, when a great deterioration set in. The Tokugawa era was one of complete peace for some two hundred and fifty years, unbroken either by revolt within or assault from without. Few dynasties can have been so fortunate and few have had stronger or abler rulers in the early stages to found and consolidate their administration. For it is a great mistake to think that Ieyasu was the only strong and capable ruler of the line. Actually of the first five Shoguns who carried on the administration until after 1700, i.e. Ieyasu, Hidetada, Iemitsu, Ietsuna, and Tsunayoshi, only the fourth, Ietsuna, was an easy-going character who did not care for ruling, with the result that an energetic and imperious minister, who was a relative, did it for him. The Shoguns had capable men about them and were well served in most things; and naturally the best of the hereditary architect-craftsmen entered their service. Of such a family was Heinai Masanobu who worked on the Nikko shrines in this capacity; his father Yoshimasa had worked on the Kōdaiji and the Toyokuni shrine where Hideyoshi was commemorated, and his grandfather Tameyoshi had built the Imperial Envoy Gate of the Jūraku mansion where he lived.

The work of this period was vigorous enough at first, but gradually everything became stereotyped and conventional, and there was no stimulus from abroad to revive it. After 1700 there was a mere repetition of detail that became weaker and more ornate in both temple and mansion, and only perhaps the Tea Masters preserved a tradition of simple elegance, though even they were by no means unaffected by the general laxity of things.

As time went on the Samurai or military class, who after 1600 or so became an hereditary caste and were forbidden to trade, became poorer and the trading class wealthier and more influential, in spite of the efforts of the government to prevent it by legislation. The result was that the soldier tended to lose his feeling for stern simplicity. Neither Nobunaga nor Hideyoshi had had time to regulate the lives of the people to the same extent as the Tokugawas, and this period is remarkable for its ever-increasing crop of detailed restrictions in the interest of economy and of the proper distinctions to be preserved between the different classes of people. Such economy and distinctions being, of course, for the benefit of the rulers. So from the great Daimyo to the small farmer their way of life came to be prescribed for them by the Gō Roju, the Great Council of the Shogun, and the houses they lived in, as well as the clothes they wore and the food they ate and the toys their children were to be allowed to play with, were carefully specified according to its views. It was all with the object of weakening any possible opposition to the dynasty and carrying out the policy of the supremacy of the Tokugawa house before everything, as laid down by the great founder Ieyasu. There had been so much civil war and general confusion for more than a century that these precautions were perhaps understandable on the principle of the proverb that "One who has been burnt will blow even on a salad." Crafts were hereditary and were strictly regulated and the apprentice had to copy exactly what his master taught him and not to depart from it on pain of expulsion. This repressed any originality though it cultivated technical skill. So the proportions of every part of a building became standardized and fixed and no great skill was required to reproduce them, which resulted in a general sameness everywhere. There was quite as much painting and carving as before, but there was a loss of freshness in these adjuncts; they were applied mechanically, so that the painting lost its decorative quality and the architecture its structural meaning.

At the same time some new types developed, such as theaters, colleges, inns, and also public baths and restaurants. There was a great improvement in domestic architecture, for the people who had never been able before to live in anything but primitive dwellings with mud walls and board floors and no ceilings now became better off under the orderly government of the Tokugawas. As their standard of living rose they built themselves more comfortable and even luxurious houses—and this in spite of legislation to hinder them, for the power of money began to make itself felt even against the privileged position of the military aristocrats and officials, who were so often in debt to the rich merchants. So as the architectural ambit had in former days passed from the temple to the great mansion, now it widened out to include the dwellings of the ordinary people.

The Tokugawa Shoguns were Lords of the Empire as no military man had ever been before them. They held a centralized administration in their hands with an increasingly tenacious grip, and the land was enmeshed in a network of rules and checks that converted it into a vast barrack system, the control of which was all concentrated in Edo. Around the Shogun's castle the Daimyos had their residences—three at least for the great lords, Upper, Middle, and Lower Yashikis, as they were called—where they lived when they were not at their castles in the provinces. For the regulation was that they should spend alternate years in each, except perhaps if they were ill, when they might be excused if the Shogun's doctors who examined them reported their indisposition to be sufficiently serious.

Encouraged as they were by the government to spend money on buildings, except fortified ones (for none might rebuild or repair his castle without permission, which was not likely to be given), their mansions and gardens were extensive and splendid. The Shogun also frequently honored them by allowing them to build or contribute to the building or restoration of some great shrine or temple, or it might be the Imperial Palace; so ever more of their income went into construction, especially as Japan is a land where fires are almost epidemic, and proverbially so in Edo. They were consequently often hard put to it for funds, "being at his shifts for money to go up to Edo," as the chief of the English factory at Hirado said of the lord of this place about the second decade of the seventeenth century.

But the country had peace and no funds were needed for war, and soon the various castle towns, which largely date from this time, became miniature replicas of Edo, even to the names of their streets.

Actually Edo itself was only a very big castle town, for Ieyasu made the same kind of capital for the country as he had had for his province, and installed the same type of government there, administering the Empire out of his own pocket just as a feudal lord did with his fief. Ieyasu had taken in hand the small castle he found in Edo when he entered it in 1590 and later resolved to make his capital there, far removed from the enervating Court atmosphere of Kyoto. With the assistance of Honda, his secretary, and Tōdō, his old friend, he reconstructed it and the town so that it was and is one of the greatest fortified areas in the world. Most of the work on it was done between 1600 and 1614, and included cutting away the top of Kanda Hill and throwing it into the sea to fill in the low-lying ground by Hibiya and make up what is now the lower or business part of the city. The higher and better part was occupied by the castle and the residences of the many Daimyos and the Shogun's own household troops and their officers (Hatamoto). Owing to its uneven site it was not possible to lay out Edo in the same regular chess-board fashion as Kyoto, though where possible the streets were made on this principle. As in other cities the various trades tended to be found together in the same streets which were called after them, Timber Yard Street, Sword Polishers' Street, Tub-makers' Street, and so on. There was a quarter where the theaters were to be found, and another where the temples of the various sects lined up expectantly to receive contributions. There was also the pleasure quarter of the restaurants and brothels which was an enclosure with only one entrance, strictly guarded and patrolled by the government constabulary and spies, because there the criminal and the revolutionary were most likely to be found and caught. When Ieyasu died in 1616 the city was much what it continued to be except for the outer moat which the third Shogun Iemitsu added—at the expense of the Daimyos, of course. It is calculated that the cost of the city to them was somewhere about the equivalent of £100,000,000.

Edo castle, the seat of the Shogun and the center of the autocratic centralized government of Japan for more than two hundred and fifty years, was of the same type as the other great castles, and had the same wide moats and massive walls and gates as Osaka. But in size few fortified cities in the world compare with it, except Peking, Constantinople, and perhaps Daulatabad.[74] There was the Hon-maru with its keep and the subsidiary wards, the Ni-no-maru and San-no-maru, in one block where the Shogun and his large family and household lived, and where the councillors and high officials came to carry on the affairs of State and the great lords repaired to pay their respects. Adjoining it, but separated by another moat and wall system, was the Nishi-maru or Western Castle where the heir to the Shogun or the Retired Shogun lived, and which also contained a large space given up to the secondary mausolea of the late Shoguns; behind this was the Fukiage park or pleasance where the inmates of the castle could enjoy all the advantages of the secluded country while living in the center of a city of a million or so inhabitants. This Nishi-maru is now the Imperial Palace.

Ieyasu, who loved simplicity and economy as, according to him, Heaven also did, was content to live in a modest style compared with that of his successors, though naturally the dignity of his office required a certain amount of ceremony and display. Hidetada, his son, did not depart much from his ways. It was in the days of Iemitsu the son of Hidetada that the architectural splendour of the period began to shine in Edo and Nikko. None of the original buildings inside Edo castle have survived, though the moats and walls and many of the towers and gates have remained unchanged and lend an air of great dignity to the Imperial Precincts. But in Kyoto the Nijō castle still preserves the great reception rooms and decoration of the time of Ieyasu, for it was erected then as an outpost of the Shogun in the old capital, from which his officials could dominate it and where he could go and stay when he himself visited the city.

The Shogun's palace was divided into three sections, the O-omote or Great Outer Palace which contained the chief reception chambers for public audience and the apartments of some officials and guards; the Naka-oku or Middle Interior which contained audience chambers for more intimate receptions of Shogunal relatives or great lords, and also the apartments where the councillors sat and met, and where the Shogun transacted the business of government; and lastly the O-oku or Great Interior tenanted only by ladies, where the Shogun retired to relax after the strenuous work of administration. Here were the apartments for the Shogun's wife and mother and his ladies-in-waiting and for all the lesser lady officials who waited on these and the maids who waited on them. It was separated from the Naka-oku by a bronze partition and specially guarded gates. None of the male officials were allowed to enter here, and communication between the inner and outer palaces was maintained by small boys. The plan of the outer palace here given has no exact date,[75] and there are two versions of it that differ in some details but have substantially the same arrangement of rooms. Since one of these has notes ascribing some of the interior decoration to Kano Tannyu (1602-1674), it may be that of the castle as it was before it was destroyed by the great fire of 1657, or of the new building put up again in 1659 in the space of six months or so.

As to the O-oku, there are two plans also that differ considerably in their arrangement. One given in the *Edo Jidai Shiron* or *Essays on the Edo Period,* issued by the Japanese Historical and Geographical Association and stated to be of the Genroku era (1638-1704), and another a copy of one by Kora Buzen, chief carpenter of the construction department of the Shogun, an office that was hereditary in the Kora family. In the second plan there is a far more regular and barrack-like layout of the suits and apartments of the ladies-in-waiting and their attendants, which are placed in long rows one behind the other called *naga-tsubone* or barrack suites. It might perhaps be the O-oku of somewhere about the year 1800.

The front or outer part of the O-oku was taken up by five separate sets of apartments which were the living and ceremonial audience chambers of the Shogun and his wife, children, and close relatives. The suites (*b*) and (*c*) were the most formal audience chambers, and (*a*) was the suite where they usually lived. The (*d*) suite is the guest suite, presumably used to receive lady connexions of the highest rank, and *(e)* consists of living-rooms. Since most of these were used by the Shogun or his wife they had dais and lower dais chambers though they were only for ceremony, and the sitting-rooms behind were actually used as living-rooms. Each suite had its dressing-rooms and bathrooms, store-rooms and antechambers. The antechamber was where the attendants sat while serving meals or conversing with those on the higher level, and the third chamber was where they retired to sit when not needed. Each of these suites with its corridors and *irikawa* (matted corridor) occupied not less than 200 mats. Next to them lay the kitchen quarters, also furnished with sitting-rooms and ante-rooms with upper and lower chambers like the rest, since on occasions they would be visited by the Shogun's wife, whose official title was Mi-daidōkoro or the August Lady of the Kitchen.[76] Beyond this again was another suite (*f*) with reception and sitting-rooms and kitchen complete. The Shogun's bathroom is described as being 12 feet by 15 feet, with a dressing-room of six mats adjoining. It was of pure white *hinoki* wood, with two tubs of white wood having green bamboo hoops on black lacquer stands for hot and cold water respectively. The decorations of all the audience chambers and other rooms were in the ornate Shōin style of lacquered wood and coffered and double coffered ceilings and gilt and painted *fusuma*, as can be seen in the Nijo palace which is the sole survivor of this type, though specimens may be seen in the ceremonial reception rooms of great temples.

Behind these suites the whole of the remaining space in the O-oku was taken up by the *tsubone* or lodgings of the ladies of various ranks who were the sole tenants of this extensive area. The larger suites for the more important lady officials seem to be situated nearest the Shogunal apartments and the smaller ones farther away. The largest have three apartments with a boarded space with kitchen, scullery, etc., and behind this the back rooms for the maids. These suites were evidently occupied by more than one lady in many cases, for it is stated that ladies attached to the Shogun had no private rooms but boarded with the seniors. The number of these senior lady officials is given as seventy-seven at the beginning of the eighteenth century. These were the officials who had the privilege of audience with the Shogun and his wife, and did not include the personal ladies-in-waiting of the latter. The total number of inhabitants of the O-oku was probably more than a thousand.

In the outer palace the Great Audience Chamber,[77] the Shiro Shōin or White Suite and the Kuro Shōin or Black Suite lay one behind the other on the left side, and behind these again the Goza-no-ma or Sitting Room Suite and the Kyusoku-no-ma or Retiring Room Suite for less formal occasions. Outside lords who were not related to the Shogun were received in the Pine Chamber, or Willow Chamber, the Tairo or chancellor in the Tamari, the Three Shogunal Branch Houses in the White Shōin, while the new year reception for the household was held in the Black Suite, and so on.

In size Edo castle stood about midway between the palace of Peking and the Seraglio of Istambul, but unlike both of these it harbored no eunuchs[78] and certainly no foreigners.

But the best known works of the Edo period are undoubtedly the shrines of Nikko. Tokugawa Ieyasu, the founder of all this peace and prosperity, had been deified after his death in 1616 as Tōshōgu Dai-Gongen, or Great Manifestation of Buddha Resplendent in the Eastern Region, and as Ancestral Deity of the actually ruling house, he was the best served deity in the country. Therefore he had to have a suitable shrine, and this was provided by his grandson Iemitsu who had the greatest reverence for his divine grandfather. Ieyasu had been buried at Kunōzan, a hill overlooking the sea near Shizouka where he died, but was transferred a year afterwards to Nikko in Shimozuke, as he had arranged before he died, or perhaps as the monk Tenkai, his spiritual adviser, had arranged after. The shrine at Kunōzan is like a miniature edition of Nikko, but is comparatively little known.

And in this way a new architectural style was created, that of the mausoleum shrine called after Ieyasu "Gongen style" and composed of a mixture of Buddhist temple, Shinto shrine, and stupa tomb. Every known type of spiritual housing was piled up to do honor to this great soldier-statesman. The shrine itself is, as before stated, modeled on the Kaisando of the Eihōji temple, or the shrines that were influenced by it like Kitano, and to this were added spacious courts like a temple, with splendid gates, bell-tower and drum-tower, pagoda, treasure house, library, stable, and every other sacred appurtenance that could be thought of. Then behind the main shrine, which consists of oratory, stone chamber, and sanctuary (Haiden, Ishi-no-ma, and Honden), and approached by long flights of stone steps, is the actual tomb, a bronze stupa pagoda of the Yugi type, with a bronze altar on which stand the usual candlestick, censer, and flower vase, the whole enclosed in a smaller court with gates of solid bronze. There is no decoration here, not a glint. The atmosphere is one of hardness and endurance, the prominent qualities of the "Divine Lord." It is a curious contrast with the casket of Hidetada, his son, whose mausoleum is at Shiba in Tokyo; for Hidetada's stupa is the same shape, but inside a shrine and very much larger, while it is covered everywhere with designs in raised gold lacquer. It is about 20 feet high and is said to be the largest piece of gold lacquer in the world. A similar shrine was built for Iemitsu beside it, and for the rest of the Shoguns, thirteen in all, there were a series of others at Shiba and Ueno in Edo at the temples of Zōzōji and Kaneiji respectively. There was another series, too, though much smaller, at Momiji-yama within the Western castle. And these latter were copied, like most other things, by the great Daimyos who had their own mausolea in their provinces, of the same type, but on a much more modest scale. Their actual tombs were not of the stupa pagoda order, but stone monuments representing the Five Elements.

It may be noted here that Imperial Mausolea have almost no architectural features, for the Sovereigns were buried in natural hills in the manner of the ancient tumulus, and this has only a fence, *torii*, and gate. The Kōdaiji temple, where the departed spirit of Hideyoshi was revered, was in some sense a mausoleum, but more in the style of the temples built for somewhat the same purpose by the Fujiwaras, as places where services might be performed that the departed great one might obtain enlightenment. But the Nikko shrines were the beginning of a new, or rather revised and adapted, cult of the deified military dictator on the lines of the deified Sovereign; for it was not long before the Shoguns petitioned for and obtained from the Imperial Court the dispatch of an Imperial Envoy every year to Nikko, thus putting it on a level with the Ise shrine of the Sun Goddess, the only other shrine to which such an honor was paid. Hidetada had built the first shrine at Nikko in 1617, but this was quite small, and the present structures were begun by Iemitsu in 1623. It took thirteen years to finish the work. The name of the chief carpenter was Kora Bungo-no-kami Munehiro, head of the Shogun's office of works, an office that became hereditary in his family. There were also two Daimyos appointed as Lord High Commissioners to be in general charge of affairs and to have authority to order anything that was needed. The buildings comprise the outer court with the Nio Gate, the middle court with the Yōmei Gate and the inner court with the Kara Gate. The Sakashita Gate leads from the second court to the tomb. In the inner court are the shrine buildings and in the others are the Kagura Stage where the sacred dance is performed before the Deity, the Goma or Fire Offering Hall, the Deity's Palanquin House, the Honchi Hall, the bell and drum-towers, the library, three storehouses, the ablution tank, the stable for the Deity's horse, and the five-storied pagoda.

The main shrine is 30 feet square, of which 12 square feet comprise the outer sanctuary (Gaijin) and the remaining 18 square feet the inner sanctuary (Naijin), within which is the Holy of Holies (Nai-Naijin). In these the work is of the finest imaginable, but they are not now accessible to any one but the ritualists and members of the family. The decoration is all of raised gold lacquer and the pillars are ornamented with overlaid work with dragon, pine, and bamboo motifs, enriched with carving and silver gilt mountings wherever possible. The connecting stone chamber, floored with granite, is 18 feet square. The Haiden or oratory is 54 by 24 feet with a space of 30 feet in the center for the main oratory, and separate ones for the Shogun and Imperial Abbot on each side of it, 12 feet wide respectively. The ceilings and other decorations of these, which are on view, are also exceedingly fine, the two side chambers being panelled with carvings of rare wood. All the pillars of these chambers and the rest of the buildings are lacquered in black and the woodwork is plastered and lacquered in gold and colors outside as well as in.

Even the floors are in black or red lacquer. The ceilings are coved and double coved and coffered with designs of birds and beasts done in gold lacquer and colors in the coffers, and everywhere there are the usual ornamental metal mounts.

The Yōmei-mon or Sun-bright Gate has often been described and more often illustrated. It is the most elaborate of all the portals. It is a two-storied gate, hipped and gabled on each of its four sides, and as complicated as such a roof can be. The construction is almost hidden by the carving in openwork, high and low relief, and in the round, that reminds one almost of a Hindu temple for profuseness, lacquered and colored from the eaves downwards. It is covered with ornamental work of every description applied wherever a place can be found for it. In all Japan there is no such riot of colored carvings. Man and all the flora and fauna are represented in it. Professor Amanuma observes, "'There is plenty to investigate in it," but he does not, I think, admire it.

All the other buildings are in the same style. Of all perhaps the canopy of the ablution tank is the most impressive, because the decoration does not detract from the construction and the line and proportion are fine. It is worthy of the plain stone tank it covers, over which the water flows evenly like a veil of crystal over all four sides. The five-storied pagoda is lacquered and painted red from top to toe, like everything else at Nikko. It was presented by Sakai Tadakatsu, a loyal councillor and relative of the Tokugawa house, and is 113 feet $3^1/_5$ inches high with a *sōrin* of 25 feet. This is only about $^1/_5$ of the total, whereas in the ancient pagodas it was about half—for example, in that of the Daigōji. Its proportions therefore are not so satisfying; but in its internal construction the arrangement of the beams and ties to ensure stability and absorb the shocks of wind and earthquake is advanced to near perfection.

Everywhere the Nikko shrines are a triumph of technical craftsmanship of the same type as was employed by Hideyoshi in the Momoyama age, but of a far more profuse and gorgeous kind. Certainly they do not compare with the splendid proportions and simple dignity of the earlier unadorned constructional work. But in a sense they are practical and efficient enough, and set in the background of dark green cryptomeria covered hills they appear less gaudy than they would on a plain. And the colors are rich and well blended. It evidently needs people who prefer black and white to manage color properly. And it must not be forgotten that their purpose was to glorify the deified founder of the Tokugawa line, certainly one of the greatest figures who ever ruled in Japan or anywhere else, who had practically become the most important Deity in the land. As propaganda for him they are successful enough, for now they attract visitors from every part of the world, as does also Taira Kiyomori's favorite shrine of Miyajima. But that is not all. With all their fine lacquer and carvings exposed to the weather they needed constant repair, and work on them has practically never ceased since the time they were built. All this had to be paid for by the Daimyos, who were granted the honor of being allowed to do it, and whose purses became more and more anaemic in consequence. Only that aspect of them may be said to represent the spirit of the economical Ieyasu, for otherwise they are according to the taste of the gorgeous and luxurious Iemitsu, the first, unapproachable autocrat of the line.[79]

His own shrine, known as the Taiyuin from his posthumous title, was begun in 1652 and was finished in about three years. Sakai Tadakatsu was the High Commissioner and Heinai Masanobu the architect. It is in just the same style as the Tōshogu, but with a difference in detail. For instance the Honden interior is like the Buddha Hall of a Zen temple with a dragon painted on the ceiling and a two-storied Buddhist shrine on the altar. Also the connecting chamber is an *ai-no-ma* (stone-floored chamber) on the same level as the Haiden. In several other points, too, it reveals Zen influence. It is therefore not exactly true Gongen style, but modified. But Iemitsu was an aesthete who was very fond of Chanoyu which has strong Zen affinities.

Beside the Nikko shrines other buildings well known to the Western world are the Great Buddha Hall of the Tōdaiji at Nara, the largest wooden building in the world, 250 feet square over the eaves and 170 feet high; the main temple of the Chionin at Kyoto and its fine Sammon; the temple of Kiyomizu, also at Kyoto; the main temple and pagoda of Asakusa in Tokyo; and the pagoda at Ueno, the only relic of Kaneiji. There are also the Kondo of the West Hongwanji at Kyoto and the gate of the Nanzenji in the same city. Of these the Tōdaiji Buddha Hall is in the Tenjiku style, a copy from Kamakura, but otherwise this style like the Kara has died out, a thoroughly mixed one only remaining; but the Wa style was known as the Shi-tennoji, and the Kara as the Kenninji after these temples.

A peculiar type of which there are few examples is that of the Mampukuji, begun by the Chinese priest Ingen in 1661, directly imported from the Ming dynasty of his country. It is of the Obaku sect of Zen and is on an extremely regular plan. There are three more of these Obaku temples in Nagasaki, of which the Sūfukuji is the finest. Their Chinese character is much more marked than is that of the Mampukuji and it is said that the great gate of the Sūfukuji was made in China and sent to Japan in pieces for erection. Most of the temples of the Tokugawa period, however, have no particular layout but are adapted to their sites. The Myōshinji at Kyoto is a fine example of a Zen temple most of which belongs to this era, though there is one part of late Momoyama origin. It is a good specimen of the regular plan of the temples of this sect and has a fine refectory and kitchen.

The Imperial Palace went on being destroyed by fire as before and then rebuilt in much the same way, but after the great Kyoto fire of 1781 the eleventh Shogun Ienari, who greatly reverenced the Imperial House, gave orders for it to be rebuilt on a very much more magnificent scale in the style of the Heian period. It was begun in 1789 and took about three years to finish. The work was under the superintendence of the great statesman Matsudaira Sadanobu, the Shogun's Premier, who took great pains in making research to discover just how the ancient palace had been arranged. But in 1854 it was burnt again and then rebuilt about three years after in the same way, and this is the present palace. Since the Emperor has now gone to live in what was the castle of the Shogun in Edo, renamed Tokyo, it is not used and can be inspected; but the Accession Ceremony must be held there, since the Imperial Castle (Kyūjō) at Tokyo does not contain a Shishinden, where alone this ceremony can be performed.

The Shūgaku Detached Palace, which can also be seen, is a spring and autumn villa presented by the Shogun Hidetada to the Emperor Go Mizu-no-ō (who designed its garden) as a country resort, and still remains in its original state.

Another type of building introduced by Tokugawa Tsunayoshi, the fifth Shogun (1681), was the Seido or College of Confucius. Confucianism was the official philosophy of the Tokugawas, and the fifth Shogun was particularly enthusiastic about it, giving regular lectures every month to the Daimyos, who thus had another tribulation inflicted on them. The Seido was a simple building in rather Chinese style and had a Hall of Confucius with a bronze statue of the sage. The example of the Shogun was naturally imitated by the Daimyos, and Confucian colleges after the same pattern sprang up in the various fiefs, where the children of the Samurai retainers were taught the Chinese classics. They were a sort of Japanese public school. That built by Ikeda Mitsumasa at Okayama was the first.

To prevent if possible the destruction of valuables by fire, the Kura or fireproof storehouse attached to temples, residences, and particularly tradesmen's shops was evolved. It is usually of two stories with very thick walls of mud covered outside with the same hard white plaster, or diagonal black tiling with white plaster joints, that was so much used for the outer walls of noblemen's mansions and those of the greater Samurai.[80] The Kura has small windows with iron shutters and a heavy door like a safe. In some cases the tiled roof is detachable. It may be connected with the house by a covered way, and in it all the pictures, pottery, lacquerware, tea utensils, books, curios and, in the case of the Samurai, swords and armor, were kept. It has had therefore a certain influence on the Japanese habit of continually changing their pictures and utensils instead of keeping them all about them in their rooms as Europeans do. It is consequently a simple matter to alter the atmosphere of a room completely by this device, especially if, as is the case in large houses, the *fusuma* are changed as well.

Edo houses were orginally roofed with wooden shingles and thatch like farmhouses, for the city developed very rapidly when, from a small town, it was suddenly promoted to be the capital of the Empire.

All the great lords had to build mansions and live there practically as hostages with many of their retainers, and it was not easy to house this sudden influx of people of all sorts very substantially. But the constant fires led the Shogun to issue an order that all dwellings should be tiled. It was the fourth Shogun Ietsuna (1660) who found Edo shingled and left it tiled.

The public bath house[81] was another institution that became popular from this time and has always remained one of the characteristic features of Japan. Hot baths and hot springs date from the Heian period or before, it seems, but the bath house business developed in the big cities. Here it in some sort performs the functions of the public house, for it is a place where all are accustomed to meet on terms of nudist equality and enliven the time with chat and humor. Its name in Edo was Sento or "one cent hot water," so it was an amusement that could be indulged in by everyone. The great, naturally, did not attend it, for they had bathrooms attached to their own residences: but the middle classes, though they often had this convenience too, went to the Yuya for the entertainment they obtained there. These bath houses consist of a large room with a place at the entrance for depositing clothes, and a high seat for the custodian on top of the partition which separates the men's side from that of the women, so that he is in a commanding position to overlook everything and take the money. A curtain may divide this part from the other portion of the room, or it may not. At the other end is the square wooden tank, usually covered in by a gabled canopy such as is seen in Hideyoshi's bathroom and called a Zakuro-guchi or Pomegranate Mouth, possibly because it spread wide and revealed everything, as that fruit is proverbially said to do.

Before long these bath houses had rooms above, where liquor and light refreshment were served by not unattractive waitresses, thus approximating more closely to a tavern or restaurant. But the government did not approve of this and prohibited them on the pretext that they would be a cause of dissipation to the Samurai; the real reason was that they were outside the pleasure quarter where amusement was government-controlled and spied upon.

The streets of Edo were furnished with gates at the cross-roads each with a guard-house (Tsuji-ban or Cross-road Guard) so that they could all be shut off should any disturbance take place, or the authorities wish to arrest any one, or the Shogun proceed through the main street which was then cleared. These gates are the proto-type, presumably of the modern police-box system. There was a very efficient force of Samurai constabulary and detectives in Edo who worked under the supervision of the two City Commissioners.

The immediate neighborhood of the castle and many other parts of the city as well were largely taken up by the mansions of the greater and lesser Daimyos with their imposing gates on the street front. And since everything in this society was regulated, the Daimyos' gates had to be built according to their standing and income, and by their shape indicated what sort of a lord lived there. It will be noted that the highest rank was shown by a pair of hipped gables on the roofs of the guard-houses that projected at each side of the entrance, and that an ordinary gable indicated a lesser rank. Lower down still the guardhouse lost its foundation and became an oriel window, while those of smaller incomes were allowed only one of these. All these fronts and gates were of plain wood after the early days, when they had apparently been often gilt and lacquered—the exception being a very great lord related by marriage with the Shogun who was allowed to paint his gate red.[82] All below the rank of Daimyo (i.e. lower than 10,000 *koku)* had to have a plain front to their gate-house without any of these projections. If a feudal mansion was destroyed by fire it was not allowed to be rebuilt as before, but in a simpler way with an unroofed gate as a penalty for carelessness. Beside the castle towers and a few pagodas the only noticeable feature of the Edo skyline was the firetower in each district which contained a bell that was rang with an increasing number of strokes to the minute in ratio of nearness to the fire.

Along the street front of the feudal mansions ran the "longhouse" barracks *(nagaya)* in which the retainers lived round their lord. They were often diagonally tiled about half way up the outside wall and were either of white plaster or black weatherboard with wooden dibs laid vertically over it above.

Of the three or more mansions a Daimyo maintained, the one in Daimyo Street (Daimyo Kōji) outside the castle gates, or near one of the other gates, was the Upper Mansion where he would stay while he had business at the castle paying calls or otherwise being in attendance, or if he held office as councillor and so on. The Middle Mansion was usually a little farther away, and so had more room for gardens and also housed the vassals of lesser importance and the family. The Lower Mansion was in the suburbs and had not as a rule such large buildings or place for many retainers, but was set in an extensive garden and used as a place of diversion away from the crowded city. The residence of the lord himself lay back across the courtyard behind the front gate, and was entered by the usual porch with pillars supporting the projecting roof of Chinese gable form over the *shikidai* or boarded platform in front of the entrance hall on which the servants knelt to receive guests, as they still do. Inside there were the same Shōin reception rooms with *irikawa* and outer veranda and dais as in the Shogun's castle, but on a much smaller scale, and varying with the means and taste of the owner.

None of these mansions has survived in Tokyo, except the Hama Mansion by the Sea; but in some of the castle towns in the country there are Daimyo mansions or villas[83] like those at Hikone, now an inn, and Okayama and Hiroshima, now public parks. The residences of the Hatamoto or Shogun's high officers were of the same type also, but smaller and simpler again, and smallest and simplest of all were those of the ordinary Samurai which, however, were still built on the same plan. In the castle towns, as in Edo, the Samurai lived in certain quarters by themselves, and apart from those of the tradesmen, artisans, temples, theaters, and amusement caterers. The smallest Samurai called *Ashigaru* or footsoldiers lived in a set of streets called Bancho or "guard quarter" like that outside the castle at Edo. Those of higher rank lived nearer to the castle, and the streets they occupied were much wider than those used for trade or amusement—a narrow street for shopping and a broad one for military pomp and strategy, a most practical arrangement. In the hot summer days the narrow streets can be covered in by drawing canvas blinds across from one side to the other, and they also lend themselves to decoration with lanterns and other devices both by night and day in a way that leaves little to be desired.

Neither the Japanese shop nor the inn has departed as much from the plan of the private house as in Europe. The shop, called *mise* (show-place) or *tana* (shelf), is merely the house front opened to the street by raising the shutters and disclosing a matted space, with an earth floor below it in the same style as a kitchen. The customers stand on the earth floor or sit on the edge of the matted part, on which squat the shopkeeper and his assistants and on which are set out samples of his goods. Behind this is the house in which the master and some of the assistants live. It is very often separated from the shop by a courtyard garden. Shops vary a good deal according to the goods they sell, but this is the general plan.

Inns, too, are only like a large private house with many rooms, and sometimes a shop front added where the guests are received and the host often sits. But the best type of inn has not even this, but only a spacious porch like a mansion. There are no public rooms, for every one feeds and sleeps in his own room as at home. The only exception is the bathroom, and that is rather more public than the bath house since there is no division for men and women. Inns very often have fine interior decorations and also beautiful gardens such as are, I think, not so often found in Europe. The same thing applies to restaurants which, when in Japanese style, hardly differ much from inns, except that they do have rooms large enough to entertain a large party of people if necessary, though smaller groups prefer to have their meals privately in separate rooms. Public drinking shops hardly exist except in the sense that roadside tea-houses that sell tea and cakes and rice to travellers also sell liquor. In fact I think anyone can sell liquor and tobacco if they wish at any hour, as on the continent of Europe, and their drinking habits are similar, so that there is nothing that one could describe as public-house architecture. The cities are not therefore disfigured, as are ours here, by the occupation of many of the best sites of the main thoroughfares by gin palaces, repellent as a rule to both eye and nose, and sometimes an embarrassment to law and order. The roadside tea-house in Japan, though it is not exactly architecture, is as well mannered as more permanent structures and rather adorns than defaces the countryside. This is apparent from the many charming illustrations in which it figures in the black-and-white illustrated guide-books to Edo, the Tokaido road, etc., called *Meisho Zue* or *Pictures of Famous Places* and published about 1800.

CHAPTER 11

The Shogun's Reception Of The Emperor

On the twenty-first day of the ninth month of the year 1438 the Emperor Go Hanazono deigned to visit the Shogun Yoshinori, who prepared four rooms on the eastern side of the Shinden for the Imperial use. Wide matting was spread on the floors and there were screens and curtains and the *mi-chodai* (a four-post canopy over the seat or bed of the master) was put there for His Majesty's sleeping chamber. The rest of the Shinden was for the Emperor's living-room suite (Tsune no Goza-sho). On the twenty-second day there was a performance of Bugaku[84] in the western court, after which His Majesty repaired to the *tai* or adjoining building and a banquet was served. Following that there was a poem-composing party that continued till late at night.

On the twenty-third there was another performance of Bugaku in the courtyard. The former performance had been given by courtiers of both the higher and also the lower ranks (those who had not the right of entering the Imperial Presence); but today only these latter took part and both the courtiers of the Imperial Suite and the Shogun and his household were graciously permitted to view it.

On the twenty-fourth it rained and nothing particular was done, only they feasted all day in the six rooms of the Shinden. On the twenty-fifth His Majesty viewed a game of football from the western veranda and then there was a banquet within the screen, after which there were parties for Japanese poems, Chinese poems, and music, given on three boats. His Majesty proceeded from the eastern door of the southern veranda to the boat on matting that was laid down by the officers of the Kamon department. The courtiers preceded him carrying lanterns and the Chujo[85] bore the Imperial Sword. The Kambaku,[86] the former Kambaku Kaneyoshi, and the Shogun and his suite were in attendance. The Emperor proceeded to the boat for Japanese poems. On it was a high pavilion with two phoenixes, and two pieces of white jade on pedestals decorated the prow. The boat for Chinese poems had a dragon figure-head and that for music had a water-fowl. And there was the man in the moon with a Chinese crown. Round the lake and on the island were cressets that lit up the scene, along the western eaves of the mansion were hung lanterns that threw reflections onto the water, and the ladies-in-waiting on His Majesty with those in attendance on the Shogun and his consort came out on the southwest veranda to see it. When the music was over they proceeded to a part at the end of the Reception Room (Go Kaisho) where a temporary Izumi Dono had been made and were entertained by recitations of Chinese poetry.

On the twenty-fourth, the day of the Imperial Return, there was a banquet in the Go Kaisho and afterwards the Shogun presented His Majesty with a writing by Ono-no-Tōfu in a golden box suspended from a golden bough by a chain of jade. Beside this both the Shogun and his consort made large presents of gold and silver and costumes, and the courtiers of the Imperial Suite and the ladies-in-waiting all received very valuable gifts.

CHAPTER 12

Building Regulations In The Tokugawa Period

AMONG the regulations of the various details of life in the Tokugawa period those about the limitation of the size and decoration of houses according to the rank and income of the individual bulk fairly large. It is probable, too, that there was more of it than appears in the published laws of the Shogunate, for much was done by local officials who had considerable power. The feudal lords issued these prohibitions when they were hard up, just as the Shogun did. In the very early days of the Shogunate there was no special legislation of this kind for the military class, and it is not until the time of the third Shogun Iemitsu that we meet with it. The farmers were no doubt too poor to need it before this, for it was the policy of the first Shogun so to tax them that they had no surplus at all—a condition, in his opinion, most conducive to hard work.

But in 1643 we find: "Those under 10,000 *koku,* even Bangashira (chief officers in a clan), must not have reception rooms more than 15 feet deep (2½ *ken).* But the kitchen may be 18 feet deep (3 *ken).* When houses are rebuilt it must be done according to this measurement." And it was not likely that any one else would have a larger one except a Daimyo whose income must be at least 10,000 *koku.* The average size of the farmer's house in early Tokugawa days was about 15 feet—that is, supposing the *ken* in which these measurements are given was 6 feet as later. But this is not quite certain, for the *ken* was 10 feet in the Kamakura age and later on was 9 and 7 feet.

Again in 1657 we find regulations for the dwellings of the people: "In building it is unnecessary to say that 'long houses' are not allowed, and living-rooms behind shops must not be more than 3 *ken* deep."

Then in 1668 there was an order about the building of temples:
(a) Three *ken* of Kyoto measure is the limit of depth, but the front-
    age may be as desired.

(b) The wing with the Buddhist shrine must not be more than three *ken* square, Kyoto measure.

(c) The lean-to veranda all round shall not be more than one and a half *ken*.

(d) The roof-ridge shall be a short one.

(e) There must be no construction above the bracketing.

No halls, guest-chambers, monks' residences, or refectory kitchens shall be longer than the dimensions given. If it is desired to make them so the matter must be referred to the Shrine and Temple Commissioner for his decision.

Regulations for residences: The following are prohibited:

(a) Frieze beams.

(b) Cedar doors.

(c) Built-in Shōin windows.

(d) Fine and rare wood.

(e) Carving, openwork, carved bracketing, or any elaborate ornament.

(f) Lacquering of the edges of the *tokonoma* or the use of Chinese paper for the sliding doors.

(g) Gates made of *keyaki* wood (*Zelkova acuminata*).

As to the temples, it appears that village temples or small ones are meant; but the rules about residences show that people were becoming comparatively well-to-do and apt to afford things that are the sign of superior rank.

In 1699 there is another order:

Those with incomes of from 3000 *koku* to 1000 *koku* are not to build houses exceeding 2½ *ken* in depth. And in future no carving, bracketing, or lacquering of the rims or beams of the *tokonoma* is allowed.

Walls set with stones are not allowed. But a *no-tsura* (rough stone wall) may be permitted where necessary.

For those below 1000 *koku* income 2 *ken* deep is the limit for rooms, and in future frieze beams, cedar doors, built-in Shōin windows, carving, bracketing, and lacquering of the *tokonoma* edges and beams, and the use of Chinese paper for the *fusuma* is prohibited.

Again in 1716 the eighth Shogun Yoshimune, who had to enforce economy where possible, because the extravagance of his predecessors and the natural limitations of the Shogunate income had brought the country into financial difficulties, issued a set of regulations limiting the size of the house to 3 *ken* deep and forbidding the use of frieze beams and detached rooms, since luxury did not conduce to good farming. This also shows how the standard of living was rising, a fact that is rather confirmed by the observation of a *shoya* or large farmer in 1730. He says: "Thirty years or so ago most peasants lived in houses with earth floors and matting laid over it. But now we see not only boarded floors as well as ceilings, *tatami,* and waist-high *shōjij* but *shikidai,* outside verandas, and landscape gardens as well."

CHAPTER 13

Shōji, Fusuma, And Ceilings

Shōji And Fusuma

The two words *shōji* and *fusuma* now mean the outside sliding doors covered with translucent paper *(akari-shōji* or light *shōji)* which are used in a Japanese room like the European French window, and the solid inside sliding doors that divide one room from another. The literal meaning of *shōji* is "interceptor" and it was first used for any sort of screen, whether sliding or standing independently. The sliding variety was known as *fusuma-no-shōji,* and the meaning of *fusuma* is "bed-quilt," a name that was given to this kind of sliding door because the pattern on it originally was like that on a bed-quilt. The word *shōji* was then dropped and these inside doors were known as *fusuma* only, and also *karakami* or Chinese paper from the material with which they were covered. The standing screen of one leaf, which was used in the Heian period before there were any sliding doors, was called *tsuitate-no-shōji,* and in the same way the word *tsuitate* is now used by itself to denote a single-leaf screen. The word *shōji* was then left to denote what took the place of the old *shitomi* or flap-gratings covered with paper, still seen in Shinto shrines and temples. The papered *shōji* is only a very much lighter version of this with wide spaces and very thin and delicate slats. The early *shōji*, as in the first half of the Ashikaga period, were only papered on their upper part, the lower being solid wood, the *koshitaka-shōji* or waist-high variety still used in kitchens. Actually they are already found in the Hakuzan shrine at Uji of the Kamakura period. A later development was to paper the whole of it to give a greater amount of light in the reception and other rooms. It was lighter in weight, too, and would slide more easily, and this quality no doubt also caused the heavy wooden sliding doors to be replaced by paper covered *fusuma*. The construction of the frames of both is much the same, but the *fusuma* is papered on both sides with thick paper. The wooden sliding door or *mairado* is still used for cupboards and other places. No doubt these heavy wooden fittings were more to the liking of the tough Kamakura warriors than to the elegant companions of the Ashikaga Shoguns, and it may be that the progress of the craft of paper-making had something to do with it.

The Ceiling

The commonest and simplest ceiling in Japanese houses is the flat one made of thin boards overlapping at the edges and laid over slender transverse rods or beams, the whole being suspended by perpendicular ties that attach it to the rafters above. It is called *saobuchi-tenjo* (rod ceiling) or, when the beams are bevelled, *saruho-tenjo* (monkey-cheek ceiling). Though extremely light and cohesive and so safe from falling in earthquakes, it has the defects that the boards are apt to curl and chinks open; the rats commit a nuisance through it and dust accumulates there, coming down, especially in an old house, like rain in a high wind. Also when the thatch has to be renewed in a thatched house this settlement of dust is particularly troublesome. And at night when the rats begin to scamper about they are apt to shake down this dust in the faces of people sleeping underneath.

The coffered ceiling, if well constructed, is not liable to these defects. It was common in the early days and came from China, but was more or less confined to temples and large residences. The ordinary house, which for long remained unceiled, never adopted the coffered ceiling but took to the simpler variety. The Japanese word for ceiling, *tenjo* (heaven's well), refers to the coffered type, for the squares on it are like the Chinese character for a well-head. The ceilings of tearooms are different in that they are often made of plaited wood or bamboo strips or of reeds, and the supporting rods are often bamboos also. Small though they are, tearooms not seldom have three varieties of ceiling together. The formal which is the Saobuchi type, the inter-mediate, of reeds etc. at a lower level, and the informal, consisting of the dressed open rafters *(kesho yane-ura)* which may be, for instance, of natural wood and bamboo alternating. But these conceits are not found elsewhere, except perhaps in a restaurant, where the uncommon and even bizarre is permissible because people do not have to live with it but only stay there for an hour or two. Generally speaking ceilings are uniform everywhere.

The reason why ceilings are rarely papered is the presence of those dwellers above them, the rats, that "are apt to do an unseemly peony on them." On this subject the famous comic poet, Shoku Sanjin, made the well-known couplet:

> *Nezumime ga Tenjo-bito no mane wo shite*
> *Shita-tare taruru Shii no Shōsho.*
> (These beastly rats are imitating courtiers
> Dropping down thus on a major-general of the Fourth Rank.)

which he composed to console a certain Daimyo who held the rank aforesaid when a rat urinated through the ceiling and spoiled his fine *shita-tare* or Court robe just as he was preparing to go and pay a visit in full dress at the Shogun's castle. There are two puns in this verse, the first *tenjo-bito* (courtiers) which could also be read "ceiling people," i.e. rats; and *shita-tare* which means both "a Court robe" and also "to drop down." However, in spite of this, ceilings are occasionally papered and decorated with writing or painting. Even the ordinary ceiling varies considerably in its value according to the fineness and evenness of the grain of the wood used in it. The grain must match and run in the same direction, so that the boards for one room must be cut from the same log.

CHAPTER 14

Privy And Bathroom

The Privy

The privy in a Japanese house is sometimes under the same roof as the other rooms near the bathroom and sometimes built out under a roof of its own, either at the end of the veranda or else at a little distance and connected by a covered way. Never, I think, does it stand like a sentry-box looking self-conscious and far from ornamental, as it is apt to do in unsewered areas in Europe. It is always architecturally part of the house, and the woodwork and finish of it should be equal to the best elsewhere. As it is often said, "the *tokonoma* and the privy need the best work." This is doubtless because guests use it and is also a legacy from the Zen point of view on the subject, which is especially apparent in that attached to tearooms. The Japanese are, it may be noted, quite lacking in that latrinophobia which characterized the nineteenth century English.

The privy has an oblong slot in the floor edged with a porcelain or celadon fitting, and underneath this is a large jar let into the ground and cemented round about, perhaps a couple of feet below the floor. This is cleaned out through an opening in the wall beside it at intervals by the peasant whose privilege it is to remove the contents to fertilize his ricefields. Next to this compartment, which is technically called Daibenjo or Great Convenience Place, there is another containing a urinal which is called Shombenjo, the Lesser Convenience Place. These two conveniences are always catered for separately in this way, no doubt in the interests of agriculture. In restaurants and elegant houses these places are extremely tasteful and in the former case may often have a miniature garden or arrangement of rocks to adorn them. It is not perhaps an ideal arrangement, but it has worked well for centuries and presumedly will continue to do so. A Japanese critic says: "There are three ways apparently of solving this problem. That of the European who goes to great trouble and expense to remove and destroy what is very valuable fertilizer. That of the Japanese who conserves it and builds a suitable and seemly place in the house to do so. And that of the Chinese who spends nothing and provides nothing, but goes out into his garden and applies it directly. Logically the last is the most economical and effective, but..." The oldest word for privy is Kawaya, which is found in the *Kōjiki* and so is not later than the eighth century anyhow, of which more than one explanation is possible. It may be for "river-house," for there is evidence that in early days these conveniences were built over a stream as they are in the Koya temples where examples may still be seen. It may be noted that these passages in the *Kōjiki* refer to the Deities of Izunio where it is quite likely the whole house was often built over the water, and examples of this are to be found in the Naka-umi lagoon of that province still.

In the section of Jimmu Tenno we read that the Great God Onamuji had changed himself into a red painted arrow and so projected himself into the channel under the privy where a beautiful damsel was. She took it home and put it by her bed and it turned into a handsome youth and so she came to bear a daughter to the Deity. Incidentally thieves not seldom enter houses this way with no necessity for any metamorphosis. Another view is that Kawaya means "side-house" because it was built out under a separate roof. Or again the word *kawa* (excreta), is explained when it is a parallel with Hi-dono or gutter-chamber. The Hi-dono was a place where wooden vessels for use as a commode were kept and used and afterwards cleansed. The word for such a vessel is still *o-kawa*. This was the style of convenience in use in the palace and in great mansions, it would appear. The maid-in-waiting who looked after it was called Mi-kawa-yōdo Hisumashi (August-flushing-maid-in-waiting). That the greatest care was taken about its cleanliness is evident from some other names for this place, e.g. Seiyōsho or Pure Clean Place and also Setsuin, the classical word, first written up over the Tōsu of the Zen temple of Kenninji at Kyoto. It is compounded of *setsu*, part of the name of a Chinese monk who found enlightenment in cleaning it out and *-in*, part of the name of his temple.

In the sixteenth century we have a detailed description of the Go-kansho or Retirement Place of Takeda Shingen the shrewd and ferocious Lord of Kai, famous both as a soldier and a scholar. It had an area of six mats (9 by 12 feet), so that Shingen would have plenty of room to maneuver if attacked there suddenly, a thing by no means unknown in those days when no scruples were observed. The drain from the bathroom next to it was led beneath it in order to utilize the waste water, so that Shingen, beside his other remarkable qualities, may also be the Japanese Harington. There was also a censer there in which fine incense was kept burning day and night by the gentlemen-in-waiting always on duty. And there Shingen had his state papers taken and would consider his decisions, and that may have been why he himself called it Yama, the mountain—of meditation.

The Bathroom

Bathrooms in residences are comparatively ancient, for there is one in the Seiryōden in the palace at Kyoto, while later on they are found in the great Zen temples and in the plans of the Kamakura military mansions. Some think that the steam bath such as is found in Hideyoshi's bathroom is the more ancient form and this may be so,[87] though hot spring baths were known and used in the tenth century (e.g. that of Dōgō in Shikoku) and hot water seems the simpler. There are no very early details perhaps, but it seems that the bathroom has not altered much since the sixteenth century.

There is a mention of a "plank bath" (*ita-buro*) in a story in the *Ima Monogatari* of about 1250, in which it is related that a monk who has some eye complaint goes to one with his eyes bandaged, and never having seen this kind of bath before mistakes a door in the street for it and proceeds to undress there, much to the amusement of the bystanders whose laughter leads him to take off the bandage and discover himself standing naked in the street.

The oldest type of bath seems to be one with an iron bottom on to which a coopered tub with bamboo bands was fitted. The bottom was set in a clay base like that of the kitchen stove and a fire of brushwood lit under it. To protect the feet from the hot bottom a wooden lid was floated on the water and the bather got on to this so that it sank with him. As the smoke was considerable, this kind of bath was usually put in an outhouse near the kitchen. It is known as Goemon-buro or Goemon bath, from the highwayman Ishikawa Goemon who was boiled in one by Hideyoshi's orders and who made a long and defiant oration from it during the process. Some twenty years ago they still existed in the country and may still do so. Another type, probably later, is that in which there is a stove built into the bath tub, which is oval in section, so that the water circulates round it like a water tube boiler. A third type has the water heated in a detached furnace and boiler outside, which communicates with the bath by pipes. This is the kind generally used in hotels and public bath houses.

The hot spring bath houses at fashionable spas are often very fine buildings that might easily be mistaken for temples, with massive and lofty tiled roofs and very imposing entrances. Others are more of the farm-house type and blend very happily with the lines of the hills and sea shore. When Japanese bathe they like to get a good view at the same time, if at all possible, and so large windows will be placed in such a way that one can sit in the bath and look out on the hills or sea. The same thing applies also to hotels which are built facing a sea view, if by the shore, or country or garden one, if inland. This may not seem very remarkable, and yet in this city of Sydney of more than a million inhabitants, set round a piece of water that is not unknown in the world, there is perhaps hardly more than one hotel or restaurant where a meal can be combined with a sea view, even at one of the well-known bathing resorts on the coast. And one of the finest sites on the harbor is used as a tramway depot, though to lend it dignity it is disguised architecturally as a fortress. It is rather reminiscent of the armored knight in the Victorian baronial hall whose belly opened to disclose a stove. Precisely the antithesis of these things is the town planning and building of Japan.

CHAPTER 15

The Kitchen

THE kitchen in a Japanese house naturally varies as elsewhere with the style and size of the building. In the country house and farm it is spacious and the boarded portion is often used as a family dining room. It is always open to the roof to prevent stuffiness from the fumes of charcoal or faggots from the stove and braziers. It is neatly and efficiently arranged for convenient access to the vessels and utensils needed for cooking and serving meals, and here it is likely that it was influenced by the Mizuya or Tea-kitchen of the ceremonial tearoom where every utensil has its exact place, thought out to conform with the principle of economy of movement, which is one of the main features of ceremonial tea-serving. So the kitchen is always next or very close to the family living-room, bathroom, and servant's room, and the isolation of these parts of the residence as incompatible with "gentility" has never come about and does not need to be corrected as in modern European styles. This is largely because the servants are all maids and are treated as members of the family. The custom was and still is that members of the social grade just one below that of the family should be employed as domestics, beginning with the Court where daughters of the Court nobility served, and the mansions of the Shogun where those of the lesser military nobles and Samurai.

In the kitchen the stove is an important object, regarded with deep respect or veneration as the source of sustenance for the house.[88] It had its tutelary Deity, like the well and the privy and the garden. Where this stove was in the covered court by the kitchen there was in the northern provinces a big odd-vizaged figure as much as six feet high up against the pillar against which the stove was placed. This was called the male pillar (otoko-bashira) and the figure, hyōtoku, which Fujita conjectures to be the same as hyottoko, the common word for "an ugly fellow," possibly from hi-otoko (fire male). Kōshin is usually the kitchen Deity, and food and drink offerings are made before him. Sometimes it seems the breakfast rice is cooked with fire lighted from the sacred flame that burns before his shrine.

The stove is built up of clay plastered over much like the setting of a copper and has sometimes one large or three, five, seven, or even nine smaller fireplaces in it, each with a hole on top on which the pot or cauldron is placed or, in the case of the large variety, inset. In Edo the stove is placed facing the earth floor of the kitchen, but in central Japan it faces the boarded part. In this region round the ancient capital the stove is also regarded as part of the house, even more so than the *shōji* and *fusuma,* whereas in Edo it is removed by the owner if he lets his house and the tenant must bring his own. In the extreme north climate has modified the kitchen, since there the open hearth, over which the pots are hung by a *jizai*[89] or suspender, has superseded the stove.

Though the stoves are often now made in a straight line, an old form that is still common in the country is the semicircular shape, by which the fire and cooking vessels are brought within easy reach of the cook without need of superfluous movement. In some old country houses there is one large stove that is unused and regarded as the sacred fireplace, while the cooking is done on a separate range. Mention of this reverence for the stove is found in the earliest records of the Nara age in the proceedings of the Palace Kitchen Department (Oi-ryo), and such observance may have derived from China where it is ancient enough, for we find in *Analects* iii, 13 the question "Is it better to pay attention to the God of the Hearth than to the ancestral shrine?" The *Li Ki* observes that the House Deity lives in the kitchen in spring, in the gate in summer, in the well in autumn, and in the garden in winter. Fujita sees a reference to this in the kitchen god he found revered in parts of Okayama province, called Odokū Sama, which he interprets as the Japanese Tsuchi-gimi or Earth Lord.

CHAPTER 16

The Architect

THE architect in the sense that we now understand the word, that is a scholarly professional expert who can design anything in any style to order, has really only been known in Japan since the Restoration of 1868 and the introduction of European ways; but the history of the constructive craftsman and artist, professional and amateur, is not so very different from what we find elsewhere. As the arts and crafts entered Japan with Buddhism it was natural that Buddhist monks and scholars should be the experts in them and the directors of construction, for they had knowledge and leisure and were able to travel on the continent. That they should have remained so was only to be expected, for right up to the seventeenth century professional men like doctors and Chinese scholars and painters were all tonsured, though that is probably as far as the religious aspect of the majority went. Zen monks were the fathers of domestic architecture and gardening, as we have seen, and they in turn produced the Tea Master who continued where they left off and became an hereditary professional aesthete in a very specialized sense. One great advantage that a monk possessed, even a nominal one, was that he was outside all social grades, since theoretically he did not belong to the world at all, and so was free to enter any society no matter how exalted, even that of "Those Above the Clouds," where only the highest Court noble might go.

In the earliest days there was the monk Dōji of the Sanron sect who studied in China for sixteen years (701-717). He brought plans from the Hsi Ming temple in China which he used to build the Daianji, one of the seven great temples of Nara. Similarly Gembo of the Hosso sect and Kanshin, Chinese monks, came to Japan and worked in the same era.

Quite as important as the designer was the craftsman or temple builder, Zōjiko ("make temple artisan"), also called Daitōryō (master carpenter), or simply Takumi (craftsman). He and his associated assistants did the work, and the skill they must already have pos-

122

sessed, judging from the workmanship of the most ancient objects, evidently enabled them to carry out anything required of them. Since the technique of wood-working does not alter, the country has always retained a large population of these artisans living simply and inexpensively, yet able to do fine work, and, owing to their long apprenticeship and hereditary craft, endowed with an eye naturally sensitive to harmony of form and balance.

Since Zen monks were even more secular in their ways than the other kinds and particularly cultivated a simple and functional manner of living as likely to lead to enlightenment, they studied the layout and details of buildings and gardens. Scholarly and versatile indeed, they would do anything for the great feudal lords, their patrons and often relatives, from planning their gardens and family temples to carrying on their dubious diplomacy when it seemed profitable and even sometimes leading their armies when it ceased to be so.

So when Hideyoshi had restored something like peace after the many wars of the sixteenth century and began to build temples and palaces, it was a monk of Mount Koya he put in charge of his works. This Mokujiki Shōnin is described as having been in charge of the buildings on Mount Koya since he was twenty-five years old and very experienced; and when Hideyoshi's great Buddha temple was being raised he built himself a little hut beside the work and did not leave it day or night. He became a great friend and confidant of the art-loving autocrat and was one of the very few permitted to attend his quiet funeral.

The Tea Master had already begun to act in the latter half of the Ashikaga period as aesthetic advisor to the Shogun and his nobles, and in their days his sphere was limited to them and to the details of etiquette. But with the rise of the famous Sen Rikyu in the days of Nobunaga and Hideyoshi, the Tea Master's influence spread to the military men and merchants and the ordinary people, and definitely affected architecture.[90]

The Tea Master was like an architect who was given a commission to design a house with its interior decoration, furniture, and garden, as well as to instruct the owner how to live in it properly. He became the arbiter of taste and the critic of pottery and pictures and stones and bamboos and all the other things that make life in the opinion of cultured Japanese. And since, like all the other arts and crafts, his business became an hereditary one and branched out all over the country, it helped to keep taste at a higher level through the Tokugawa period than might otherwise have been the case. The house of Sen Rikyu still flourishes and now in the fourteenth generation remains unique in the aristocracy of aestheticism.

Among these Tea Masters the most famous for his creations in building and garden planning was Kobori Masakazu (1579-1647), usually known as Kobori Enshu because his title was Lord of Tōtōmi, which is commonly abbreviated thus. His family was a military one and he had an income of 10,000 *koku* per annum, while he acted as Chief of the Board of Works for the Shogun's mansion and also as Commissioner of Fushimi, an administrative position in the government. He was distinguished in all the arts, painting and poetry, flowers and tea, and connoisseurship of antiques. Very many fine gardens are ascribed to him, and as he was the teacher of the Shogun Iemitsu for tea and his advisor on art matters generally, none had more influence in these things, especially as Iemitsu was an enthusiastic art patron as well as a great autocrat. He was in some sort a Japanese edition of Sir John Vanbrugh born a few decades after his death, but the light and delicate work he has left is as great an antithesis to the massive ostentation of the latter as well can be. The retired Emperor Go-Mizu-no-ō, who died in 1680 aged eighty-five, was also a great expert in building and garden planning as well as a distinguished man of letters.

Since the work of a Japanese building can so safely be left to the master carpenter and is so largely standardized, it is very easy to be an amateur architect, and their number has always been large. Particularly do retired people, whose hobby is often Chanoyu, interest themselves in building or rebuilding parts of their houses and making tearooms and gardens. And though the buildings are standardized in their measurements there is plenty of variety in detail and in the arrangement of the buildings on the site and the relation of the rooms to the gardens. Since there is no finality about the building of a Japanese house, and it is not a squarish block dumped on the middle, or at one end, of a piece of land, there is always opportunity for amusement for the owner and the carpenter in adding another section or a detached room in the garden.

Mention should be made, too, of the famous artist Honami-Kō-etsu, whose pottery and lacquer are so well known even in the West, and who is renowned in Japan as one of the greatest calligraphists and artists. He designed and laid out a village for himself and all his craftsmen to live in, on a charming site at Takagamine outside Kyoto. There was no art in which he did not excel; indeed, he was an amateur of them all, for his profession was that of hereditary sword connoisseur to the government, for which he was paid quite a comfortable salary.

Later on, about 1800, there was the Daimyo Matsudaira Fumai, lord of the province of Izunio, the most outstanding figure among the feudal nobles of his day, who was not only a very able administrator of his fief but a great Tea Master and connoisseur and writer on aesthetic matters. He was a fine amateur architect and designed his garden at Ozaki outside Tokyo with its numerous detached villas and tearooms.[91] He was blessed with a master carpenter named Kobayashi Jōdei, of extraordinary skill, who was quite a wizard in any kind of woodwork and in Europe would no doubt have been called a great sculptor. In Japan he was just an artisan, eccentric in his behaviour and a great toper, but otherwise quite content to carry out his master's designs.

It was Matsudaira Fumai who restored and added to the Kōhōan villa in the Zen temple of Daitokuji at Kyoto, built by Kobori Enshu as a retreat for his retirement. This great monastery is the Pantheon of eminent aesthetes, many of them dictators and statesmen as well, and most of their memorial chapels are worth a visit.

The hereditary master carpenter to the Shoguns, Kōra Buzen-nokami or Lord of Buzen had a nobleman's title, a privilege he shared with all swordsmiths whose craft was naturally the most appreciated; but these were honors only and carried with them no noble status or income. And practically all buildings were built by these craftsmen, supervised on occasions by their employers or by some Tea Master or amateur aesthete.

So the reason why in Japan an architect can be dispensed with, and yet the labor of the builders be not in vain, is primarily because Japanese structures are put up with a view not to their outside appearance but to their function. The roof is the only part that may be impressive. It may be noted, too, that there is no monumental architecture in Japan—with some exceptions that are copies of Occidental work. No statuary is found commemorating the great, though the longest avenue in the world was planted in honor of one of them. The tombstone is but a neat slab to hold an inscription and the great lord had only a conventional stupa. Imperial tombs are natural hills overgrown with trees. The idea of calling great men or events to remembrance by useless and expensive piles of stone has not occurred to the Japanese. Neither have gardens ever contained statuary or fountains consisting of figures that vomit water. This latter seems quite a Western idiosyncrasy, for neither India nor China nor even Egypt knows of it.

The landscape garden with its conventionalized natural scenery is really a more important part of the composition than the house, since the latter is but the shelter from the weather from which to look at it. So it follows that a garden planner is more essential than an architect, for when the garden is made the craftsman has only to put the house into it as seems most fitting. This process must, of course be modified in crowded streets and business premises, in which the courtyard gardens are apt to be embraced by the buildings; but the feeling is not different. It is, in fact, the garden maker who is really the architect, who "adds use to beauty and space to strength," but not by any means the gardener. He has nothing to do with it, and thus the result is very much the antithesis of the builder's house in the seed-shop gardener's garden that practically without exception greets the eye in this island continent. For the Japanese garden is made to supply shade and coolness and privacy and quiet, as well as a living picture from the house through the whole year; it is not a small nursery or a place for the competitive growing of flowers.

APPENDIX 1

Professor Amanuma's Illustrations Of Japanese Architecture
(*Nippon Kenchikushi Zuroku*)

THIS appendix contains the page numbers and list of plates in Professor Amanuma's *Illustrations of Japanese Architecture* (*Nippon Kenchikushi Zuroku*). It may serve the double purpose of identifying the photographs in the four volumes of this work for those who wish to consult it but do not read Japanese, and also of providing a comprehensive list of historic Japanese buildings according to their successive epochs.

Asuka Period (552-645 A.D.)

Page

Vol. I

3	Izumo shrine
4	Sumiyoshi shrine
5	Ise great shrine, Honden
6	Atsuta shrine
7	Hōryuji temple
8	Middle gate and pillar bases
9	side view
10	eaves
11	balustrade
12-13	Kondo
14	stylobate
15	eaves
16-19	details of roof
20-3	bracketing
24	doors
25	interior brackets
26	balustrade
27	Pagoda
28-9	altar details
30-1	pinnacle
32-3	balustrade
34-5	spire and finial
36-9	Cloister
40-3	roof details
44-7	Shitennōji, Osaka
48-9	Kondo
50	Hokkiji, pagoda
51	Eaves
52	Hōrinji, pagoda
53	Eaves and finial tile
54-5	Stone pagodas, Sakuragawa village, Shiga prefecture
56-65	Hōryuji, Tamamushi shrine

Nara Period (645-794 A.D.)

Early Period, 645-709 A.D.

68-73	Kairyuōji, model pagoda
74-7	Yakushiji, pagoda

Later Period, 709-794

Tōdaiji

90-1	Reconstruction of Nandaimon
92	cloister
93	pagoda
94	middle gate
95	Buddha hall

APPENDIX 1

96   Tengai gate
97-111 details of brackets roofs and
        tiles
112   Hokkedo
113-19 details of roofs brackets and
        altar base
120-1   Library
122-3   Shōsōin, treasure-house
124-9   Shin-Yakushiji, Hondo
130-1   Kairyuōji, Sai Kondo
132-41 Toshōdaiji, Kondo
142-3   Kōdō (lecture hall)
144-7   Hōryuji, east gate
148-51 Library
152-7   Refectory and loggia
158-61 Tōin Dempōdō
162-5   Yumedono
166-7   Taimadera
168-71 East and west pagodas
172-5   Eisanji, octagonal hall
        (Hakkaku-endo)
176   Internal roof construction
177-9   Designs on canopy and tie-
        beams
180-7   Stupa carvings, stone
        stupas, pillar bases, and
        stone finial tiles of this
        period

Heian Period (794-1185)
Early Period, 794-897 A.D.
190-4   Murōji, pagoda
195-200 Kondo
206   Mount Koya, site of great
        pagoda
207   Negoroji Dai Dempōin,
        pagoda (rebuilt 1515)
208   *Right*, Metal Yugi pagoda,
        Hōryuji

        Left, Yugi pagoda stupa
        shrine, Manseiji temple,
        Togano, Osaka
209   Picture of Yugi Daishi,
        Ryukoin temple,
        Mount Koya
210   Yugi pagoda rebuilt at
        Ryukoin, Mount Koya,
        by Professor Amanuma
211   Sorinto at Enryakuji, Hieizan

Later Period, 897-1185
214   Daigōji, pagoda
215-22 Detailas and decoration of
        Ohara Sansenin temple,
        Hondo
223-5   Ōjō Gokurakuin
226-61 Hōōdo of Byōdōin Uji
262-7   Amidadō of Hokkaiji
268-70 Joruri-dera, Hondo
271-3   Yaku-shido of Kami-daigo
        temple
274-9   Hōryuji, Saiin belfry
280-5   Daikōdō
286-93 Kakurinji, Daishindo
294-5   Jōkōdō
296-9   Hakusui, Amidadō
300-1   Kōzōji, Amidadō
302-7   Chusonji, Konjikidō
308-9   Fukutokuan, Hondo
        (Nagano)
310-13 Sambutsuji, Nageiridō
314-15 Fukiji, Daidō
316-18 Wall paintings at Kōchi
        before and after restoration
319   Yakushidō
320-3   Stone stupas
324-5   Demon tiles
326-7   Kasuga shrine, Nara

328-9   Usa shrine
330   Kamo shrine, Kyoto
331   Hiyoshi shrine, Sakamoto
332   Uji shrine

Kamakura Period
(1185-1392 A.D.)
Wayo Style
Vol. II
1-71   Rengeō-in, Hondo
         (Sanjusangen-dō)
72-83   Kyō-ō Gokokuji (Tōji),
         details
84-5   east gate of Kanchoin
86-7   log built treasury
88-93   Daihonji, Hondo
94-7   Nembutsuji, Hondo
98-105   Daigōji, Kondo
106-9   Iwabunedera, pagoda
         (3 story)
110-15   Kumihama Hongwanji,
         Hondo
116-27   Kōdaiji, pagoda (Tahōtō)
128-31   Kaijusanji, pagoda (4 story)
132-3   Monju hall
134   Hōjōji, Nio gate
135   Hondo and covered water
         tank
136-7   Interior shrine
138-52   Daifukkōji, Hondo
153-8   Pagoda (Tahōtō)
160-5   Byōdōin, Kwannon hall
166-9   Gokurakuin, Hondo
170-2   Kōfukuji, Hokuendo
173   Hōryuji, Saiendo
174-5   Jūrinin, Hondo
176   Tōdaiji, Hokkedo
177-9   Akadana (projecting
         ablution chamber)

180   Reido (prayer hall)
182-7   Ai-no-ma (middle chamber)
188-9   Chozuya (washing place)
190-1   Shin Yakushiji, east gate
192-3   Bell-tower
194-6   Toshōdaiji, drum tower
197   Shariden and Reido
         (reliquary and prayer hall)
198-201 Yakushiji, Tōindo
202-13   Chōkyuji
214-25   Hōryuji, Seirenin
226-7   Sankyoin
228-34   Toin, Shariden (reliquary)
235   painted chamber
236-7   Chōgakuji, Gochido
234-49   Taimadera, Mandara hall
250-1   Murōji, Kanchodo, before
         and after restoration
252-5   Kondo
256   Daiyakuji, Hondo
257   Daishido
258-9   Enjōji, pagoda (3 story)
260-7   Ishiyamadera, pagoda
         (Tahōtō)
268-74   Saimyōji of Ikedera (Kora
         village, Shiga prefecture)
275-7   Kongorinji, Hondo
278-87   Kōōnji, Kwannon hall
288-91   Jiganin, Kondo (Hineno
         village, Osaka)
292-7   Pagoda (Tahōtō)
298-307 Shōjōin, Hondo
308-15   Kongo Sammaiin, Pagoda
         (Tahōtō) built by Masako,
         oldest Tahōtō with
         Ihiyarna, 1222
316-19   Library (log built)
320-33   Kongobuji, Mount Koya,
         Fudo hall, 1197

334-41 Chōhōji, Hondo
342-53 Pagoda (Tahōtō)
354-79 Mirokuji, Hondo (Sugano
 village, Hyogo prefecture)
380-9 Jōdōji, Hondo (Onomichi,
 1226)
390-7 Pagoda (Tahōtō)
398-409 Daisanji, Hondo
410-11 Ishide temple, gate (near
 Dōgō hot spring, Iyo)
412-15 Pagoda (3 story)
416-17 Bell-tower
418-29 Hondo
430-3 Jōkaiji, Hondo (Inazawa
 village, Aichi prefecture)
434-7 Stupa shrine
438-41 Ryuzanji, gate (Tokiwa
 village, Aichi prefecture)
442-49 Hondo
450-1 Chusonji, Konjikido (Oido,
 1120 and 1222)
452 Reizanji, Hondo
453 Toshōdaiji, Kōdō, altar
454-5 Hōdōji, altar (Ikoma
 village, Nara)
456 Tōdaiji, Hokkedo, shrine
 base
457 Shin Yakushiji, Hondo altar
458-60 Kongoji, Hondo, pillarbases

Kara Style
Vol. III
1-13 Fusaiji, Buddha hall
14-21 Umeda, Shaka hall
22-35 Ankokuji, Shaka hall
 (Tomo Port.)
36-51 Shinkakuji, Hondo (Nishi
 Ono village, Oita
 prefecture)

52-61 Eihōji, Kwannon hall
 (Tajimi town, Toki district,
 Gifu prefecture 1314)
62-85 Kaisando
86-93
94-103 Tenonji, Buddha hall (built
 by Ashikaga Yoshimitsu,
 1312 Toyotomi village,
 Takada district, Aichi
 prefecture)
104-12 Suadera Ietomi town,
 Ashikaga, city Tochigi
 prefecture)

Tenjiku Style
114-33 Daigōji, Library
134-44 Tōdaiji, Nandaimon
145-52 Kaisando (Pounder's hall
 called also Ryobendo or
 Ryoben hall from name of
 founder)
153-5 Bell-tower
156-70 Jōdōji Jōdō hall (Ono town,
 Hyogo prefecture)

Composite Style
172-8 Kanshinji, Hondo

Shinto Shrines
180-1 Tamate-yori-matsuri-
 kitaru-sakatoki shrine (log
 built house for the Sacred
 Car; Oyamasaki village,
 Kyoto prefecture)
182-3 Hakusan shrine, Uji
184-9 Mitamaya shrine, Kamo,
 Kyoto
190-2 Uji Kami shrine, (upper
 shrine), Haiden

195	Uji main shrine
196-7	Saga shrine, Yamagi village Kyoto
198-207	frog-crotches
208-13	Enjōji Kasuga Hakusan shrine
214-15	Itsukushima shrine
216	Site of Eikyuji temple, Kara
217-27	Ishigami shrine, Haiden
228-37	Uda Mizuwake shrine, Kyoto
238-51	Shinra Zenshindo shrine
252-5	Mikami shrine (Shiga prefecture), Haiden
256	Gate
257-65	Honden
266-9	Kasuga shrine (Oishi village, Omi)
270-1	Ono shrine (Konze village, Shiga prefecture), gate
272-4	Oshidate shrine (Shiga prefecture)
275-86	Tate Mizuwake shrine (Akasaka village, Osaka)
287-95	Sakurai shrine (Niwatani village, Osaka prefecture)
296-303	Jōdōji temple, Hachiman shrine, Haiden
304-5	Itsukushima shrine, Marōdō shrine, Harai-dono
306-16	Honden
317-78	Stone pagodas, stupa pagodas, reliquaries, and pillars
380-91	Demon-faced finials
393-5	Futaiji temple (Nara), south gate
396-406	Giant frog-crotch

MUROMACHI PERIOD (1362-1570 A.D.)

Vol. IV

3-6	Kaenji Kinkakuji, Kyoto
7-10	Gishōji, Ginkakuji, Kyoto
11-12	Tōkyudo
13-17	Manjuji, Aizen hall, Kyoto
18-21	After typhoon of 1934
22-9	Tōfukuji temple, Sammon gate
30-9	Inner decoration of Sammon gate
40-9	Tōsu or Necessarium
50	Bath house, exterior
51-6	interior
54-5	vapor baths
57-8	Hōtōji temple, Kyoto, pagoda Tahōtō)
59-65	Suonan temple, Tanabe (Kyoto), Hondo
66-9	Enjōji (Yagyu village, Nara), gate
70-1	Hōryuji, gate
72-3	Tōin, cloister
74-6	Zuika-in temple, Hirano village, Nara
77-87	Kimbu-senji temple, Yoshino
88-97	Fudōji temple (Shimoda village, Shiga prefecture), Hondo
98-101	Chōhōji temple (Hamanaka village, Wakayama), gate
102-5	Hōonji temple (Iwakura village, Wakayama), Hondo
106-13	Yakushi hall
114-21	Dai-Dempo-in (Negoro, Wakayama), pagoda (Tahōtō)
122-37	Kakurinji temple, Hondo

138-9 Altar
140-5 Shrine eaves
146-54 Jōdōji temple, Hondo
155-61 Shrine details
162-77 Myōō-in temple (Kusado village, Hiroshima prefecture)
178-97 Fudō-in temple (Ushida village, Hiroshima prefecture)
198 Kōjōji temple (Setoda town, Hiroshima prefecture)
199-209 Pagoda (3 story), 1442
210-17 Tōzenji temple (Hiyoshi village, Imaharu, Ehime prefecture), Yakushi hall
218-21 Shrine
222-7 Kōryuji temple, Hondo
224-5 Peculiar capitals
228-9 Sempukuji temple (Toyosaki village, Oita prefecture), Kaisando
230 Jōkōji temple (Shinano village, Aichi prefecture) Hondo
231-5 Altar
236-45 Anrakuji temple (Bessho village, Nagano prefecture), pagoda (octagonal)
246-9 Taihōji temple (Urasato village, Nagano prefecture), Kwannondo shrine
250-3 Kokubunji temple, pagoda (3 story)
254-60 Enshōji temple (Miyoshi village, Nagano prefecture), Shaka hall
261-3 Altar
264-5 Pagoda shrine, 1502

266-71 Enyūji temple (Hikin town, Tokyo prefecture), Hondo
272 Jizo hall (Hibashi village, Fukushima prefecture)

Shinto Shrines

274-83 Daigoji temple, Seiryudo, Haiden
280-1 Shitomi and early *shōji*
284-93 Kuse shrine, Kyoto
294-7 Suido shrine (Terada village), Kyoto
298-315 Soraku shrine (Soraku village, Kyoto), friezes and frog-crotches
316-21 Danzan shrine, Sakurai pagoda (only wooden 13-story pagoda in Japan)
322-5 Monjuin Hakusando (Abe village, Nara prefecture)
326-41 Jishu shrine (Katsuragawa village, Shiga prefecture)
342-6 Katte shrine (Kagamigawa village, Shiga prefecture)
347-59 Yuhi shrine, (Yuhi village, Shiga prefecture), carved figures of dancers, 1493
360-3 Hachiman shrine (Ono village, Kyotani Hyogo prefecture), frog-crotches
364-9 Kibitsu shrine (Ichinomiya village, Okayama prefecture)
370-91 Itsukushima shrine (Hiroshima prefecture)
392-405 Ima-Hachiman shrine (Yamaguchi city)
406-17 Hachiman shrine (Hachiman village, Aichi prefecture)

418-27   Koshio shrine (Omagari
             town, Akita prefecture)
428-9   Hachiman shrine (Jogo
             village, Yamagata
             prefecture)
430-2   Dewa shrine (Toge village,
             Higashi-tagawa district,
             Yamagata prefecture),
             pagoda (5 story)

Devil-face Finial Titles, Inscriptions etc.
434-43   Hōryuji, Nandaimon tiles

MOMOYAMA AND EDO PERIODS
(1560-1600A.D.)
Vol. V
2   Kyōō Gōkokuji (Tōji)
             monastery, Nandaimon
3   Nandaimon, side view
4-7   gable
8   Kondo
9-12   details
13-15   altar
16   Hiunkaku villa, Nishi
             Hongwanji monastery
17   Boat entrance
18-19   Interior
20   Dais chamber
21   Corridor
22   Bathroom shelf
23   Entrance gable
24   Great Hail of Audience
25   dais
26   dais alcove
27   frieze
30   Haku Shōin reception
             chamber, corridor
31   dais
32-5   details of dais

36   Kuro Shōin reception
             chamber, exterior
37   corridor
38-9   irikawa
40   interior
41-5   shelves
46-7   Kiyomizu temple
48   Balustrade
49   West gate

Daitokuji monastery
50-1   Imperial Envoy's gate
52-61   upper story details
62   Karamon gate
63-96   details

Daigōji Temple
97   Imperial Envoy's gate
98-9   Samboin, front Shōin
             reception chamber
100   cool pavilion
101   pavilion ceiling
102-3   corridor of front Shōin
104-7   Shinden reception chamber,
             window, shelf, and frieze
108   Site of pagoda (now burnt)
109   Gotai hall (now burnt)
110-17   details
118   Kokubunji temple, Sendai,
             Yakushi hall
119-22   Details
123-6   Altar details
127-8   Matsushima, Gotai hall
129-33   Interior shrine
134   Zuiganji temple,
             Matsushima
135-9   Middle gate
140-1   Onari-mon
             (Shogun's gate)

ZUIGANJI TEMPLE, MATSUSHIMA
142-3   Main hall, porch
144-5   gable
146-7   side view
148-51   details
152-61   interior details
162-71   Outer corridor details
172-83   Main hall and details
184-7   Risshakuji temple
         (Yamadera village,
         Yamagata prefecture),
         middle hall and details

Edo Period Temples
189-91   Kyōō Gōkokuji (Tōji)
         pagoda
192-6   Kiyomizu temple, Kyoto
197-9   Chionin temple,
         Sammon gate
200-1   upper story details
202-5   Nanzenji temple,
         Sammon gate
206-8   Mampukuji temple,
         front gate
209   Manjuin gate
210-17   Sammon gate
218-21   Tōdaiji temple,
         Daibutsu hall
220-4   Kongobuji temple
         (Mount Koya), Yakushi
         and Ihai halls
225   Yakushi hall, eaves
226-9   porch
230   ceiling
231-6   altar
237   Sufukuji temple (Nagasaki),
         Sammon gate
238-43   Dai Ippo gate
244-51   Gōhō hall

252-63   Great hall
264   Fukuzaiji temple
         (Nagasaki), middle gate
265   Stone struts of middle gate
266-9   Front hall
270-88   Main hall
290   Shitennōji temple (Osaka),
         pagoda (blown down,
         1934)
291   Tennōji temple (Shitaya,
         Tokyo), pagoda
292   Asakusa Kwannon temple
         (Tokyo), pagoda
293   Hōsenji temple (Nakano,
         Tokyo), pagoda
294-9   Zōzōji temple (Shiba,
         Tokyo), San Gedatsu gate
300-1   Rinnōji temple (Nikko),
         main hall
302-3   Sōrinto pillar
304-5   Chōshōji temple (Hirosaki),
         gate
306-16   Saishōin temple (Hirosaki),
         pagoda
317-20   Jionji temple (Daigo village,
         Yamagata prefecture)

Momoyama Period Shrines
322   Mizuwake shrine
         (Yoshino), gate
323-31   Main hall
332-9   Iido shrine (Kumoi village,
         Shiga prefecture),
         main hall
340-3   Itsukushima shrine,
         Miyajima subsidiary
         shrine
344-9   Hachiman shrine
         (Hakozaki), gate

350-4   Munakata shrine (Tajima village, Fukuoka prefecture), main hall Sumiyoshi shrine (Sumiyoshi, Fukuoka prefecture), main hall

356-67 Hakuzan shrine (Handa town, Nagano prefecture)

368-82 Ozaki Hachiman shrine (Sendai city), main hall

Edo Period Shrines

384-7   Iwashimizu Hachiman shrine (Kyoto), hall of offerings (Heiden)

388-93 Outer hall

394-5   Corridor interior

396-9   Kashiwabara shrine (Yamato), oratory (formerly the Naiji-dokoro of the Imperial Palace, Kyoto)

400-2   Kashii shrine (Fukuoka), main hall

403-8   Iwakizan shrine (Iwaki village, Aomori prefecture), gate

409-12 Oratory

Torii of the Momoyama and Edo Periods

414-15 Hakozaki shrine

416-17 Itsukushima shrine, Miyajima

419   Omiwa shrine, Omiwa, Nara

Edo Period Bridges

420-1   The Kure covered bridge at Usa Hachiman shrine, Kyushu

Edo Period Mausoleum Shrines

423   Tōshōgu shrine (Nikko), torii and front gate

424-5   Torii

426-33 Pagoda

434-5   Stone chamber, corridor detail

436-48 Western corridor details

450-67 Main hall

468-9   Taiyuin shrine (Nikko), main hall, interior

470-1   Kōka gate

472-3   Bronze gate of inner mausoleum

474-6   Stupa pagoda of inner mausoleum

Momoyama Period

478-81 The two stone mausolea before the inner shrine, Mount Koya

Momoyama and Edo Periods

484-504 Tiles

APPENDIX 1

SUPPLEMENT
Nara Period to Edo Period (725-1870)

Page	Temple	Period
2-11	Yakushiji temple, eastern pagoda, details	Muromachi
12-21	Ichijōji temple, pagoda	Muromachi
22-4	Jōruri temple, pagoda	Nara and Heian
25	Kōryuji temple, Keiguin octagonal hall	Kamakura
26-7	Tōfukuji temple, Gekka gate (from Imperial Palace)	Kamakura
28-35	Jōdōji temple (Harima)	Kamakura
36-47	Jōddōji temple (Onomichi), Amida hall and stupa pagoda	Kamakura
48-67	Kōryuji temple, main hall	Muromachi
68-71	Shakusonji temple (Kawabe village, Nagano), Amida hall and inner shrine	Heian
72-5	Zensanji temple (Nishi Shiota village, Nagano), pagoda	Kamakura
76-85	Hōtōji temple, gate and stupa pagoda	Muromachi
86-99	Buttsuji temple (Takasaka village, Hiroshima prefecture), Jizo hall	Muromachi
100-3	Dōshunji temple (Yamaguchi city), Kwannon hall	Muromachi
104-11	Rurikōji temple (Yamaguchi city), pagoda	Muromachi
112-13	Tōfukuji temple (Yamaguchi city), main hall	Muromachi
114-25	Yakushi hall	Muromachi
126-137	Jōunji temple (Iwaki village, Ehime prefecture), Kwannon hall	Muromachi
138-145	Ankōkuji temple (Kofu village, Gifu prefecture), library	Muromachi
146-158	Honkokuji temple (Kakinomoto town, Kyoto), library	Momoyama
159-167	Shomanin temple (Yuigaoka town, Osaka), stupa pagoda	Momoyama
168-175	Honkyoji temple (Amagasaki town, Hyogo prefecture), founder's hall	Muromachi
166-181	Shinnyodo temple (Kyoto), pagoda	Muromachi
182-193	Kurodani temple (Kyoto), Sammon gate	Edo
194-9	Ninnaji temple (Kyoto), pagoda	Edo
200-22	Shitennōji temple (Osaka), Kondo	Edo

HEIAN TO MOMOYAMA PERIOD (800-1570)

Page	Shrines	Period
224-5	Uji-kami shrine, main hall	Heian
226-8	Ichijoji temple, Goho hall	Kamakura
229-31	Myoken and Benten halls	Kamakura
232-43	Furukuma shrine (Yamaguchi city)	Muromachi
244-63	Hirashimizu Hachiman shrine (Hirakawa village, Yamaguchi prefecture)	Muromachi
264-6	Soe-mikata-ni-imasu shrine (Tomio village, Nara prefecture)	Muromachi
267-9	Dazaifu shrine, Shiga shrine	Muromachi
270-5	Yugi shrine (Kurama village, Kyoto)	Momoyama
276-87	Suwo shrine (Hongo village, Nagano prefecture)	Momoyama
238-93	Itsukushima shrine, Miyajima Toyokuni shrine	Momoyama

MOMOYAMA AND EDO PERIODS
Detached Palaces

295-307	Nijo detached palace (Kyoto)	Momoyama
308-317	Katsura detached palace (Kyoto)	Momoyama
318-331	Shūgakuin detached palace (Kyoto)	Edo

Residences

333-9	Residence of Yoshimura Hikojiro	Momoyama
340-1	Residence of Furui Yoshiya (Kumadori village, Osaka)	Momoyama
342-3	Frieze of reception room in Jōdōin Temple, Uji	Momoyama
344-5	Frieze of reception room of residence of Motoide Tsuminosuke (Oi village, Ehime prefecture)	Edo

Tearooms

347-50	Saihoji temple (Kyoto), Shonantei tearoom	Momoyama
351-62	Minase shrine (Shimamoto village, Osaka), tearoom	Edo

Castles

364-403	Himeji castle, Harima	Momoyama

Tiles

405-32	

Comparative Table Of Dates

India	China	Korea	Japan
B.C.			
663-543 Age of Buddha	551-479 Confucius		660 Jimmu
322 Maurya Empire			Tenno.
273 Asoka			Early
200 Indo Greek Rulers of Gandhara			period
122 Chinese journey to India	20 Han dynasty	Three dynasties: Koguryu, Kudara, Silla	
A.D.			
20 Scythian Kushan dynasty			
120 Kanishka	221 Three kingdoms		
320 Gupta Empire Hindu renaissance			
405-11 Travels of Fa Hien in Indi	420 Wei dynasty North and South kingdoms		
455 White Huns	581 Sui dynasty		540 Asuka period
606 Harsha Vardhana of Kanauj	618 T'ang dynasty		640 Hakuho period
629-645 Travels of Hiuen Tsang			
660 Rajput kingdoms			720 Tempyo period
		935 Koryu dynasty	780 Heian period
	907 Five kingdoms		
	960 Sung dynasty		
1175 Muhammedan Turkish kingdom of Delhi	1127 South Sung dynasty		1190 Kamakura period
	1206 Yuan dynasty		1340 Muromachi period
1526 Mogul Timurids	1368 Ming dynasty	1392 Yi dynasty	1570 Azuchi-Momoyama period
			1616 Edo period

Glossary of Architectural Terms

相間　　*Ai-no-ma,* stone-floored chamber.

明障子　　*Akari shōji,* translucent sliding door.

雨戸　　*Amado,* rain door.

蟻頸　　*Ari-gashira,* dove-tail (ant-head).

蟻溝　　*Ari-mizo,* dove-tail socket (ant-channel).

校倉　　*Aze-kura,* log-built storehouse.

四阿　　*Azumaya,* hipped roof building.

便所　　*Benjo,* privy.

暈　　*Bokashi,* shading off.

仏壇　　*Butsudan,* buddhist shrine.

仏殿　　*Butsuden,* buddha hall.

屏風　　*Byōbu,* folding screen.

千鳥破風　　*Chidori hafu,* dormer.

違棚　　*Chigaidana,* irregular shelves.

千木　　*Chigi,* projecting rafters.

棕　　*Chimaki,* tapering pillar.

帳臺　　*Chōdai,* a curtained seat or bed.

勅使門　　*Chokushi-mon,* Imperial Envoy gate.

中段　　*Chudan,* middle dais.

中門　　*Chūmon,* middle gate.

臺所　　*Daidokoro,* kitchen.

大工　　*Daiku,* carpenter.

臺輪　　*Daiwa,* wall plate.

大斗　　*Daito,* pillar capital.

大塔　　*Daito,* great stupa pagoda.

出丸　　*Demaru,* barbican

土臺　　*Dodai,* foundation stone.

土間　　*Doma,* earth floor.

海老虹梁　　*Ebi kōryō,* lobster tie-beam.

海老束　　*Ebi tsuka,* lobster brace.

縁側　　*Engawa,* veranda.

吹寄椎　　*Fuki-yose taruki,* clustered rafters.

袋棚　　*Fukuro-dana,* hanging shelf.

舟肘木　　*Funa hijiki,* boat-shaped elbow bracket.

風呂場　　*Furoba,* bathroom.

風呂屋　　*Furoya,* public bath house.

衾障子　　*Fusuma shōji,* opaque sliding doors.

襖　　*Fusuma,* opaque sliding doors.

蒲団　　*Futon,* sleeping quilt.

伽藍　　*Garan,* monastery (Samgharama).

外陣　　*Gaijin,* outer sanctuary.

下段　　*Gedan,* lower dais.

懸魚　　*Gegyo,* verge-board (suspended fish).

玄関 *Genkan*, entrance hall.

擬宝珠 *Giboshi*, balustrade pillar-head.

五重塔 *Gōjū-no-tō*, five-story pagoda.

格天井 *Gō tenjō*, coffered ceiling.

破風 *Hafu*, gable.

拝殿 *Haiden*, oratory.

八角堂 *Hakkaku-dō*, octagonal hall.

鼻隠 *Hana-kakushi*, beam nose cover.

梁 *Hari*, cross-beam.

梁間 *Harima*, depth of a building.

柱 *Hashira*, pillar.

法堂 *Hattō*, instruction hall.

瓶束 *Heisoku*, king post.

竈 *Hettsui*, kitchen stove.

肘木 *Hijiki*, elbow capital.

引手 *Hikite*, door push.

広小舞 *Hiro-komai*, wide lath.

廂 *Hisashi*, a lean to.

桧皮葺 *Hiwada-buki*, hinoki shingled roof.

方形 *Hōgyō*, pyramidal roof.

方丈 *Hōjō*, monks' residence.

宝珠 *Hōju*, upper bulb on pagoda spire (pearl).

本殿 *Honden*, main shrine.

本瓦 *Hongawara*, true tile.

本丸 *Hon mom*, main ward of castle.

宝塔 *Hōtō*, small stupa pagoda.

柄 *Hozo*, tenon.

井戸 *Ido*, well.

井桁 *Igeta*, well-head.

入側 *Irikawa*, matted corridor.

入母屋 *Irimoya*, hipped-gable roof.

爐 *Irori*, hearth.

板間 *Itama*, boarded floor.

板支輪 *Ita shirin*, boarded soffit, or cove.

泉殿 *Izumi dono*, cooling pavilion.

地袋 *Jibukuro*, cupboard on the ground.

地貫 *Jinuki*, tie through base of pillar.

上段 *Jōdan*, upper dais.

城郭 *Jōkaku*, castle.

城下町 *Jōka machi*, castle town.

壁 *Kabe*, wall.

蟇股 *Kaerumata*, frog-crotch strut.

鏡板 *Kagomi-ita*, large panel.

鏡天井 *Kagami tenjō*, panelled ceiling.

廻廊 *Kairō*, cloister.

開山堂 *Kaisandō*, founder's hall.

筧 *Kakeki*, gutter spout.

框 *Kamachi*, frame or front beam, as of *tokonoma*.

竈 *Kamado*, kitchen stove.

鴨居 *Kamoi*, grooved lintel.

要 *Kaname*, hinge.

唐破風 *Kara-hafu*, Chinese gable.

唐紙	*Karakami*, opaque sliding doors.
唐様	*Karayō*, Chinese style.
笠木	*Kasagi*, capping beam.
頭貫	*Kashira-nuki*, tie through head of pillar.
火頭窓	*Katō-mado*, ogee arch headed window.
堅魚木	*Katsuo-gi*, cross balk on shrine ridge.
厠	*Kawaya*, privy.
茅葺	*Kaya-buki*, reed thatch.
建築師	*Kenchikushi*, architect.
化粧屋根裏	*Kesho-yame-ura*, dressed roof lining.
桁	*Keta*, beam or wall-plate.
桁行	*Keta-yuki*, frontage of building.
几帳	*Kichō*, curtain.
切り目緑	*Kirime-en*, veranda with boards at right angels to building.
切妻	*Kiritsuma*, gable.
階	*Kizahashi*, staircase.
勾配	*Kōbai*, slope of roof.
木鼻	*Kobana*, beam nosing.
拳鼻	*Kobushi-bana*, fist-shaped beam nosings.
杮葺	*Kokera-buki*, shingled roof.
小舞	*Komai*, laths under tiles or plaster.
金堂	*Kondō*, golden hall.
鼓楼	*Kōrō*, drum-tower.
虹梁	*Kōryo*, tie-beam.
腰障子	*Koshi-shōji*, half-panelled *shōji*.
腰貫	*Koshi-nuki*, tie through middle of pillar.
火燵	*Kotatsu*, quilt warming hearth.
小屋梁	*Koya-bari*, roof-beam.
小屋束	*Koya-tsuka*, roof tie.
釘隠	*Kugi-kakushi*, nail cover.
組入天井	*Kumi-iri tenjō*, grated ceiling.
雲形肘木	*Kumogata hijiki*, cloud-shape elbow bracket.
倉	*Kura*, fire-proof storehouse.
榑縁	*Kure-en*, veranda with boards parallel with house.
庫裏	*Kuri*, refectory kitchern of monastery.
刳形	*Kurigata*, moulding.
九輪	*Kurin*, nine-ringed pagoda spire ornament.
廚	*Kuriya*, kitchen.
櫛形窓	*Kushigata mado*, comb-shaped window.
経蔵	*Kyōzo*, sutra library.
疎棰	*Mabara-daruki*, rafters set wide apart.
舞良戸	*Mairado*, ribbed wooden sliding doors.
巻斗	*Makito*, bracket capital.

APPENDIX 3

招屋根 *Maneki-yane*, lean-to continued over ridge (beckoning roof).

斗形 *Masugata*, pillar capital.

枡形 *Masugata*, castle gate.

廻縁 *Mawari-en*, veranda round a room.

門 *Mon*, gate.

物置 *Mono-oki*, store-room.

母屋 *Moya*, main building.

流造屋根 *Nagare-zukuri-yane*, continuation lean-to (cat-slide).

流 *Nagashi*, kitchen sink.

長押 *Nageshi*, frieze beam.

内陣 *Naijin*, inner sanctuary.

中坪 *Nakatsubo*, inner court.

海鼠瓦 *Namako-gazvara*, convex joint-tile, imbrex "bêche-de-mer" tile.

海鼠壁 *Namako-kabe*, convex plaster joint of diagonal tiled wall.

納戸 *Nando*, bed-room, store-room.

根太 *Neta*, floor joist.

西丸 *Nishi-no-maru*, western ward of castle.

野天上 *No-tenjō*, plain boarded celling.

軒 *Noki*, eaves.

軒唐破風 *Noki kara-hafu*, Chinese gable on caved roof.

貫 *Nuki*, tie.

濡縁 *Nure-en*, "wet veranda," without rain-doors.

塗 *Nuri*, lacquer.

大引 *Ō-biki*, sleeper joist.

尾 *O-daruki*, projecting rafter-end.

扇棰 *Ōgi-darwki*, fan rafters.

鬼瓦 *Oni-gawara*, devil-face tile.

鬼板 *Oni-ita*, devil-face finial.

大奥 *Ō-ōku*, great interior.

折上天井 *Ori-age tenjo*, coved ceiling.

押板 *Oshi-ita*, movable *toko-no-ma*.

欄間 *Ramma*, open-work frieze.

欄干 *Rankan*, balustrade (of important building).

櫺子 *Renji*, lattice window.

輪蔵 *Rinzō*, revolving sutra library.

炉 *Ro*, hearth.

露盤 *Rōban*, nectar pot on summit of roof.

廊下 *Rōka*, corridor.

六角堂 *Rokkarudō*, hexagonal hall.

廊船楼 *Rōsenrō*, covered corridor bridge.

龍舎 *Ryūsha*, lower bulb on pagoda pinnacle, "dragon's lair."

三門 *Sammon*, two-storied temple gate.

桟唐戸 *San-karado*, panelled Chinese door.

142

竿縁天井　*Saobuchi tenjō*, raftered ceiling.

四斗　*Sarato*, echinus of capital.

指肘木　*Sashi-hijiki*, elbow mortised through pillar.

猿頬天井　*Sarubō-tenjō*, ceiling with beveled beams.

里内裏　*Sato dairi*, rural palace.

鞘間　*Saya-no-ma*, passage room. Irikawa.

正門　*Seimon*, front gate.

銭湯　*Sentō*, public bath house.

雪隠　*Setsuin (or Setchin)*, privy (classical).

舎利殿　*Shariden*, relic hall.

鴟尾　*Shibi*, kite-tail roof finials.

渋　*Shibu*, persimmon juice varnish.

七堂伽藍　*Shichido goran*, seven hall monastery.

重樋　*Shige-darwki*, double-tiered rafters.

漆喰　*Shikkui*, plaster.

錣葺　*Shikoro-buki*, gableroof with eaves all round, "helmet curtain roof."

寝殿　*Shinden*, palace style residence.

支輪　*Shirin*, cove of ceiling or soffit.

下塗　*Shita-nuri*, under coat of plaster.

蔀戸　*Shitomi*, hanging lattice window.

褥　*Shitone*, sleeping quilt.

書院　*Shōin*, study, military mansion style residence.

障子　*Shōji*, papered sliding doors.

鐘楼　*Shōrō*, belfry.

総門　*Soman*, front gate of temple.

相輪　*Sarin*, spire of a pagoda.

層輪塔　*Sōrintō*, pillar-shaped stupa.

縋破風　*Sugaru hafu*, lean-to gable.

水煙　*Suien*, spray-like open-work ornament of spire.

簀　*Sunoko*, bamboo veranda, or seat.

須弥壇　*Sumidan (or shumi-dan)*, Buddhist altar.

手挟　*Tabasami*, rafter strut.

対屋　*Tai-no-ya*, wing of Shinden mansion.

匠　*Takumi*, craftsman, carpenter.

溜　*Tamari*, ante-room.

多門　*Tamon*, long building on castle rampart.

棚　*Tana*, shelf, shop.

椽　*Taruki*, rafter.

畳　*Tatami*, floor mat.

畳縁　*Tatami-heri*, floor mat edging.

畳表　*Tatami-omote*, floor mat surface.

亭　*Tei*, pavilion.

天竺様　*Tenjikuyō*, Indian style.

天守閣 *Tenshu-kaku,* castle keep.

手摺 *Tesuri,* railing.

飛梁 *Tobi-bari,* bearer beam, transtrum.

戸袋 *To-bukuro,* shutter box.

床柱 *Toko-bashira,* pillar of *tokonoma.*

床の間 *Tokonoma,* alcove for pictures.

枓栱 *Tokyo,* bracket capital.

斗枡 *Tomasu,* measure-shaped capital.

鳥居 *Torii,* shrine portal.

棟梁 *Tōryō,* master carpenter.

東司 *Tōsu,* privies, of a monastery.

遠侍 *Tōzamuai,* outer retainers' chamber.

局 *Tsubone,* court lady's chamber.

衝立 *Tsuitae,* single leaf screen.

附書院 *Tsuke shōin,* projecting window by a *tokonoma.*

妻戸 *Tsumodo,* double swing doors.

詰組 *Tsume-gumi,* clustering brackets.

繋虹梁 *Tsunagi-kōryo,* curved collar beam.

釣殿 *Tsuri dono,* fishing pavilion.

釣木 *Tsurugi,* suspender beam.

繧繝 *Ungen,* shading colors.

鵜の毛通し *U-no-ke tōshi,* middle verge board of a gable.

上塗 *Uwa-nuri,* upper coat of plaster.

藁葺 *Warabuki,* straw thatch.

藁座 *Waraza,* socket for pivot-hung door.

渡殿 *Wata dono,* covered way.

渡廊 *Waiari-rō,* covered corridor.

和様 *Wayō,* Japanese style.

櫓 *Yagura,* tower.

屋形 *Yakata,* mansion (nobleman).

遣戸 *Yarido,* sliding doors.

屋敷 *Yashiki,* residence of Samurai or Daimyo.

浴室 *Yoku-shitsu,* bathroom.

四足門 *Yotsu-ashi mon,* four-pillared gate.

湯殿 *Yu-domo,* bathroom.

遊郭 *Yūkaku,* pleasure quarter.

湯屋 *Yuya,* public bath house.

座蒲団 *Zabuton,* kneeling cushion.

柘榴口 *Zakuro-guchi,* bath canopy.

座敷 *Zashiki,* reception room.

禅堂 *Zendo,* meditation hall.

厨子 *Zushi,* small shrine.

Bibliography

JAPANESE WORKS

Amanuma Shunichi, Professor, *Nippon Kenchikushi Zuroku* (Illustrations of Japanese Architecture). 6 vols. Kyoto, 1934.

Amanuma Shunichi, Professor, *Nippon Kenchikushi-yo* (Essentials of Japanese Architecture). 2 vols. Tokyo, 1928.

Amanuma Shunichi and Fujiwara Giichi, *Kyoto Bijutsu Taikan Kenchiku* (Survey of the Fine Art of Kyoto—Architecture). Tokyo, 1933.

Architectural Photograph Society, *Kenchiku Shashin Ruiju,* Collection of Architectural Photographs; volumes on Gates, Ceilings, Fences, *Shōji* and *Fusuma,* Garden Gates and Garden Houses, Shrines and Temples etc. Tokyo, 1915.

Bukkyo Bijutsu (journal of Buddhist Art). Nara, 1924.

Fujii Kōji, Professor, *Nippon no Jutaku* (The Japanese Residence). Tokyo, 1928.

Fujita Motoharu, *Nippon Minka-ski* (History of the Japanese Dwelling House). Tokyo, 1928.

Fujiwara Kinsato, Jukaisho (An Historical Miscellany, c. 1460). Tokyo, 1906.

Fukui Yoshinaga, *Wafu Kenchiku Zōzō* (The Construction of Japanese Buildings). Tokyo, 1929.

Hattori Shokichi, *Nippon Ko Kenchikushi* (History of Ancient Japanese Architecture). Kyoto, 1926.

Hiraide Kojiro, *Nippon Fuzokushi* (History of Japanese Customs). Tokyo, 1896.

Ikeda Chujiro, *Daiku-jutsu* (The Art of the Carpenter). Tokyo, 1928.

Imperial Government Railway Department, *0 Tera Mairi* (Temples to be Visited). Tokyo, 1922.

Imperial Government Railway Department, *Kami Mode* (Shrines to be Visited). Tokyo, 1933.

Ishizaka Zenjiro, *Ikeda Mitsumasa-kō Den* (Life of Ikeda Mitsumasa, Feudal Lord of Bizen). Tokyo, 1932.

Japanese Academy, *Ruiju Kinsei Fuzokushi* (History of Customs of Recent Times). Tokyo, 1908 (first edition, 1854).

Kaga Shōun-kō (Life of Maeda Tsunatoshi, Feudal Lord of Kaga).

Kenchiku Zasshi (Journal of the Institute of Japanese Architects).

Kōji Ruien, *Jukyobu* (A Catena of Ancient Matters, volume on Residences). Tokyo, 1912.

Kaneko Kentaro, Viscount, *Kuroda Jōsuiden* (Life of Kuroda Jōsui, Feudal Lord of Chikuzen). Tokyo, 1995.

Masuyama Shimpei *Nippon Kenchiku Jidai Yoshiki Kanshiki Zushu* (Illustrated Review of Periods and Styles of Japanese Architecture), Tokyo, 1926.

Mitsuhashi Shairo, *Riso no Kaoku* (The Ideal Residence). 2 vols. Tokyo, 1912.

Nakazawa H. and Others, *Kinai Kembutsu,* (Sights round Kyoto). Tokyo, 1911.

Nippon Rekishi Chiri Gakkai (Japanese Historical and Geographical Society), *Azuchi Jidai Shiron* (Historical Essays on the Asuchi Period). Tokyo, 1915.

Nippon Rekishi Chiri Gakkai, *Edo Jidai Shiron* (Historical Essays on the Edo Period). Tokyo, 1915.

Ono Hitoshi, *Kinsei Jōka Machi no Kenkyu* (Studies of the Castle Town of Recent Times). Tokyo, 1928.

Orui Shin and Toba Masao, *Nippon Jōkakushi* (History of Japanese Castles). Tokyo, 1937.

Saito Kamekichi, *Toko Tana Shorn* (Alcoves, Shelves and Shōin). Tokyo, 1926.

Sato Tasukeru (revised by Professor Amanuma), *Nippon Kenchikushi* (History of Japanese Architecture). Tokyo, 1926.

Takahashi Tatsuo, *Matsudaira Fumai Den* (Life of Matsudaira Fumai, Feudal Lord of Bizen). Tokyo, 1917.

Tanaka Manitsu, *Unjo Hitsuroku,* (Mysteries above the Clouds. An Account of the Imperial Court). Tokyo, 1916.

Tayama K. and Nakazawa H., *Onsen Shuyu,* (A Tour of Our Hot Springs). Tokyo, 1922.

Toba Masao, *Edo Jo no Ima Mukashi* (Edo Castle as it Was and Is). Tokyo, 1928.

WORKS IN EUROPEAN LANGUAGES

Cram, Ralph Adams, *Impressions of Japanese Architecture;* the first edition of 1905 reprinted without alteration.

The first book in English on Japanese architecture as a whole, including sculpture. Its style makes it very pleasant to read; but had it been revised no doubt some things in it would have been altered.

Hideto Kishida, Professor, *Japanese Architecture.* Tourist library, Japanese Government Railways, Tokyo, 1935.

An excellent concise and comprehensive introductory survey of the subject: written, as are all the volumes of this series, by an eminent authority.

Japan Times and Mail, Architectural Japan, Old and New, by various architectural experts; 1936.

Dealing with all aspects of architecture and building right up to the present day. Profusely illustrated with fine photographs and plans of every kind of structure, from the temples and tearooms of former days to the many blends of traditional and modern functional forms evolved to meet the needs of the commercial, educational, entertainment, and religious habits that the post-Meiji age has developed. Town-planning and earthquake damage are included also.

Jiro Harada, *A Glimpse of Japanese Ideals,* 1937.

Lectures on Japanese Art and Culture. Chapters on Architecture, the Shōsōin, Gardens, Archaeology, Crafts etc. Finely illustrated.

Jiro Harada, *The Lesson of Japanese Architecture.* London, 1937.

Dr. Harada's books are very well written and beautifully illustrated and it would be quite impertinent to criticize them. In this and also in his earlier work (the *Studio* spring number for 1918 on Japanese Gardens) he explains his subject very clearly and shows how the house and garden form a complete framed composition.

Morse, Professor, E.S., *Japanese Homes and their Surroundings,* London, 1888.

The pioneer work in English on the subject, and even now the best—though long out of print. The author, who was Professor of Zoology in Tokyo, has also written two other works of great interest, *Japan, Day by Day,* recently reprinted, and *Glimpses of China and Chinese Homes,* both illustrated by the author's pleasing black-and-white sketches.

Noritake Tsuda, *A History of Japanese Art.* Tokyo, 1936.

Has many good photographs of the exteriors of famous buildings as well as of their interior decoration, with critical discussions. This is, on the whole, the best and handiest book on Japanese art and craft.

Seiichi Taki, Professor, *Japanese Fine Art.* Tokyo, 1931.

Has a section on "The Characteristics of Japanese Architecture" which gives a very good summary in its sixty-odd pages.

Taut, Bruno, *Houses and People of Japan.* Sanseido, Tokyo, 1937.

A book of the same type as that of Morse, but not, I think, so good; for the author, though a professional architect, has not the same experience and knowledge of the country. But his insight and appreciation make it one of the books worth reading.

Tetsuro Yoshida, *Das Japanisches Wohnhaus,* Tokyo, 1936.

This is quite a masterly and authoritative description of the dwelling house, illustrated by fine photographs and plans, admirable for those who read German, but also useful for those who don't, for the illustrations have much to say.

Tsuyoshi Tamura, Dr., *Art of the Landscape Garden in Japan.*

Another work that is indispensable to those who would understand the garden setting of the house, which can hardly be illustrated without giving most instructive views of the latter. The same may be said of the book on Japanese Gardens corresponding to that on Architecture in the Tourist Series, by Professor Matsunosuke Tatsui.

PLATES